DRINK
LIKE A
BARTENDER

— SECRETS FROM —
THE OTHER SIDE OF THE BAR

When to order top shelf and when to pass ✳ Which liquors you should
have in your home bar ✳ When to shake and when to stir ✳ How to
order like a pro ✳ Which drinks will make a bartender judge you...hard

THEA ENGST & LAUREN VIGDOR

ADAMS MEDIA
New York   London   Toronto   Sydney   New Delhi

Adams Media
An Imprint of Simon & Schuster, Inc.
57 Littlefield Street
Avon, Massachusetts 02322

First Adams Media hardcover edition AUGUST 2017

ADAMS MEDIA and colophon are trademarks of Simon and Schuster.

For information about special discounts for bulk purchases, please contact Simon & Schuster Special Sales at 1-866-506-1949 or business@simonandschuster.com.

The Simon & Schuster Speakers Bureau can bring authors to your live event. For more information or to book an event contact the Simon & Schuster Speakers Bureau at 1-866-248-3049 or visit our website at www.simonspeakers.com.

Interior design by Sylvia McArdle
Interior images © Kosta Gregory

Manufactured in the United States of America

10 9 8 7 6 5 4 3 2 1

Library of Congress Cataloging-in-Publication Data
Engst, Thea, author. | Vigdor, Lauren, author.
Drink like a bartender / Thea Engst and Lauren Vigdor.
Avon, Massachusetts: Adams Media, 2017.
LCCN 2017015063 | ISBN 9781507204115 (hc) | ISBN 9781507204122 (ebook)
LCSH: Cocktails. | LCGFT: Cookbooks.
LCC TX951 .E58 2017 | DDC 641.87/4--dc23
LC record available at https://lccn.loc.gov/2017015063

ISBN 978-1-5072-0411-5
ISBN 978-1-5072-0412-2 (ebook)

To our families, whether by blood or whiskey: we love you.

CONTENTS

INTRODUCTION

Bars are the center of the universe. Okay, they're not, but sometimes they feel like they're the center of our universe. A lot of life happens in bars. People celebrate their victories and mourn their losses. They meet their significant others. They argue over politics or plan revolutions. Bars are where people hide with their best friends and wait out the zombie apocalypse, or hitch a ride to Alderaan on "the ship that made the Kessel Run in less than twelve parsecs."

Bars are our homes away from home. A bar is our living room and we want you to be comfortable and enjoy yourself while you're here. Sit back, kick your shoes off (please don't actually take your shoes off—that's a health code violation), and have a good time. But in order to relax and really enjoy yourself, you're going to want to be able to order a drink without fear of judgment (or fear of accidentally ordering something undrinkable). That's where this book comes into play. We're here to hold your hand and make the ordering and drinking part as easy as possible, because we all know the drinking part isn't really why you're at the bar. You're there because the zombies attacked and you really just didn't have any other ideas.

Before we get started we've got to get something out of the way. There exists a common misconception that bartenders and servers are all lazy young people who can't find a "real" job. Please don't be fooled. Don't be that guy. In reality, many of us in the bar industry have one or more advanced degrees or have previously worked in a variety of careers. For the most part, we choose to do what we do for a living out of love, not necessity.

Bartending is an art, and like any other skill, it takes practice, passion, and patience. If you think bartending is as simple as just walking behind the bar and shaking some ingredients together, then we dare you to try it and see for yourself. (On second thought, we'd just have to clean up after you—how about you take our word for it instead?)

Bartending is an exciting and social job, and take it from us, when your bar is busy and your service is on point, it's a high akin to winning a sporting event (we don't get out in the daylight much, so we're just assuming here). There's something innately satisfying about having a physical, tangible product that shows your hard work. Combining raw ingredients into something new and exciting and then sharing that finished product with the world (or lucky patron) is incredibly gratifying. It's old-school alchemy and it's a huge reason why we do what we do.

In the following pages we'll share some of our favorite tips, tricks, and techniques that we've learned in our years behind the bar. There's so much evolution in the bar industry that there's always something new to share. Here's our number-one secret: Want to know how to get on your bartender's good side (beyond a well-deserved tip)? Treat your bartender with respect and they'll treat you with respect right back, *and* give you great service. It's really just that simple.

THE BASICS

Before we tell you how to create your bar at home, we'll start with telling you how we create ours at our establishments. Our guiding principles for setting up a bar are very basic: speed and efficiency. Because, let's be honest, even though you know we're crafting a drink for you with love and quality ingredients, you (and everyone else) still want that product to be made and served in a timely manner. Although every bar is different, there are a lot of elements that are pretty standard throughout the industry. And like the guys in *A Clockwork Orange*, we even have our own language that we use when we're together.

FOR THE RECORD

Let's just get this right out in the open: we love
booze. We love creating new drinks and trying
new flavors. Mixing a cocktail is an art form
these days, so much so that it's hard to
imagine that cocktails were first invented
as a way to mask the taste of low-quality
liquor. Today we have the luxury of mixing
bitters, fresh juices, and well-crafted liqueurs
and spirits to make balanced beauties we can
be proud of. We've come a long way from
shutting our eyes and chugging moonshine for
a buzz—our forefathers would be proud.

LESSON 1: THE WELL
(a.k.a. the Speed Rack)

This probably doesn't come as much of a surprise, but bars sell alcohol. Between cocktails and shots and beer and wine, we need a lot of bottles behind the bar. At our bar, we have approximately 140–160 bottles stacked on any given day. You have to be prepared, right? How many of those do we use during a shift? About ¼–⅓.

That's where the well comes in. Otherwise known as the speed rack, the bar's well is where a bartender keeps all their most reached-for bottles, from liquors to the specific ingredients on their cocktail menu. The order of the well depends on the menu and the bar, but at any bar, you'll find the first row is: vodka, gin, rum, tequila, whiskey.

So the next time you order a drink and it seems like the bartender has the ingredients right in front of them, just waiting to be used to create a drink specially for you, remember: we're not mind readers, we're just super prepared. Well, also, we're mind readers.

BARTENDER SAYS

"Hospitality is never losing the perspective that while your bar is familiar and routine for you, it is the bright spot in a guest's day and you are responsible for creating that shine. Hospitality is the ability to put yourself in someone else's shoes and meet them where they are in that moment—whether that moment is good, bad, or neutral—then taking what you are given and improving on it in a small, or perhaps a big, way."

—*Ándrea Pentabona, Bar Manager at Uni, Boston, MA*

BAR LINGO

Before you flag down a bartender (actually, please don't flag us down—we know you are there and will take your order as soon as we're free. Promise!), here are a few essential ordering terms you should lock away in your brain.

WHEN YOU ORDER:

Up: Your cocktail will be served in stemmed glass (think of it as up, so literally up and off the counter).

Down: Your cocktail will be served in a rocks glass, a.k.a. Old Fashioned glass (think of it as down, therefore low to the ground).

On the Rocks: Your drink will be served with ice. (Feel free to stipulate only a couple of cubes. The more ice you have, the more diluted the drink becomes, and if you're not going to drink the cocktail or spirit fast, it could water down the drink.)

Neat: Your drink will be served without ice. This is typically only used when ordering a straight spirit, like a whiskey neat, not a cocktail. If you have sensitive teeth or plan to drink slowly and are ordering a cocktail that may have ice, definitely clarify with the bartender. That's an easy modification!

Dirty Ice/Rocks: This means the bartender will use the ice they've stirred or shaken the drink with in your actual drink. Often people ask for "dirty rocks on the side." If you do this, your bartender will put the ice in an Old Fashioned glass with a spoon next to the cocktail. You can then add ice that has been "marinated" in the drink as you like.

Highball: A specific drink made with a spirit mixed with soda. For example, a rum and Coke is a highball, but rum with a splash of Coke is not. This is also a term for the glass the drink is served in, a.k.a. a Collins glass.

OBSCURE (BUT COMMON) DRINK INGREDIENTS

First rule of trying something new: do not be intimidated! Most likely you'll find a few ingredients in a cocktail description that you've never heard of. They may sound good, but if you've never had them before, there's a decent chance you may not like the drink. To avoid "order regret," remember that there's no shame in asking your friendly bartender for an explanation. I know what bitters are because I'm a bartender, but I don't expect you to know.

- ▶ **Bitters:** Bitters are a high-proof tincture made by soaking various herbs, flowers, spices, roots, and barks in a high-proof alcohol. Typically, bitters are only used in small doses because they are expensive and strong in taste. However, when used in higher portions, they can be truly fabulous. (Try a Trinidad Sour!)

- ▶ **Vermouth/Fortified Wine:** Made by soaking herbs, flowers, and spices in wine, and then fortifying with a spirit. Vermouths and fortified wines have been around for ages. Our favorites come from Chambéry in France. Oui!

- **Amaro:** An Italian bitter liqueur. It comes in all sorts of colors and variations. From fernet, which is heavy in licorice and bitter, to the bright, orange flavor of Aperol, amaro offers a beautiful and wide array of flavors to mix with, sip, or shoot. Some of them, such as fernet, Montenegro, or Cynar, are also great for shooting after a big meal. They're categorized as "digestifs," which means they'll help you digest your food.

- **Chartreuse:** How much time do you have? Chartreuse comes from a supersecret recipe made by French monks starting in 1737, over a century after they came upon François Annibal d'Estrées's original recipe. That's right, it took them 100 years to perfect the recipe, and that's just how perfect Chartreuse is. It can be either green or yellow. Green is stronger in taste and alcohol than the yellow, and it came first. There is also V.E.P. (Vieillissement Exceptionnellement Prolongé) Chartreuse, which is the same Chartreuse recipe, but it has been aged extra long in oak barrels. It's expensive and divine, so it's totally worth the paycheck you fork over to get it.

Fun fact! The color chartreuse was actually named after the spirit, not the other way around.

COMMON GLASSES YOUR DRINK MIGHT BE SERVED IN

Highball Glass

Old Fashioned Glass

Pint Glass

Red Wine Glass

Margarita Glass

White Wine Glass

Cocktail Glass

Collins Glass

Coupe Glass

BARTENDER SAYS

"Green Chartreuse is proof the devil exists,
and she's delicious."

—*Chris Duggan, Account Specialist at
Magic Hat Brewing Company, South Burlington, VT*

WHAT TO ORDER WHERE

Here's a list of what to order at different types of establishments. Sure, it's okay to be adventurous, but within reason! For example, if you're in the mood for a delicious cocktail, it wouldn't be the smartest decision to go to your local dive bar.

- ▸ **Pub or Tavern:** Beer and traditional pubs are a classic pairing, but there are a lot of great "gastropubs" out there that put a lot of effort into their wine list and offer glass pours that pair well with their food. Also, if the bartender looks like they know their way around a mixing glass, nothing beats a Manhattan in a cozy pub.

- ▸ **Brasserie:** Despite the fact that *brasserie* is literally French for "brewery," we find ourselves often craving red wine with casual French comfort foods. At any rate, Steak Frites tastes equally good with a glass of Bordeaux or a robust porter.

- ▸ **"Family" Style Restaurant:** Stick to draught beer or highballs. Cocktails tend to be made with overly sweet artificial "mixers." Don't trust anything billed as a "Top Shelf Long Island Iced Tea."

- ▸ **Fine Dining:** We like to start off with a cocktail or a glass of something bubbly, then move to wine with dinner.

- **Farm to Table:** Cocktails made with local produce, local beer, local wine, local anything are your best bet.

- **Speakeasy:** Cocktails. Only cocktails. Either classics or something off the house list.

- **Nightclubs or Music Venues:** A highball or a beer. Something the bartenders can make quickly that you can easily carry around while dancing/moshing/casually leaning against a pillar. Be prepared for it to be served in a plastic cup.

- **Brew Pub:** Draught beer...c'mon.

- **Casual but Trendy:** Look at the menu for context clues. If the cocktail list has a lot of house infusions and house-made ingredients, go for a cocktail. If there are more than a dozen beers on tap, try one!

- **Sports Bar:** Beer is king when paired with fried snack food. We'll even go so far as to recommend a lager, IPA (India pale ale), or Pilsner, but go with something refreshing that suits your taste.

- **Dive Bar:** Bottle or canned beer, possibly with a straight spirit (a brand you trust) to sip alongside of it. Well spirits tend to be cheap, and if it's a particularly dirty dive bar (some of our favorites) the draught lines probably don't get cleaned as often as they should.

- **Any International Cuisine:** When in doubt, stick with what that region is known for!

BARTENDER SAYS

"I don't order filet mignon at a pizza joint.
Don't order a Sazerac at a dirty rock club."

*—Nicole Jaquith, Bartender at The Middle East Restaurant,
Cambridge, MA*

BAR LINGO

Daywalker: If you hang around a bar long enough (bartenders love company!), you might hear a few things you don't usually hear in the real world. For example, we try very hard not to refer to anyone as a customer. If anything, you are our guest, someone we've invited into our creation and home away from home. We've got regulars, who, just like Norm on *Cheers*, frequent our establishment to become part of our squad. Then there are the daywalkers.

See, when you spend as much time working at night as bartenders often do, you sometimes forget what it's like in the daylight. Therefore, guests who work a regular 9–5 job or aren't in the industry are sometimes referred to as daywalkers. It's not an insult, it's a fact. We are people who work all night, sleep late, and then stay up late. We are, therefore, not daywalkers. We struggle to get to the bank before it closes, we can't remember the last time we made it to a brunch, and our friends stopped asking us to go away on the weekend long ago.

86: We're out of it. If you pay attention, you will hear this on a busy night. For example: "86 Lunazul Blanco, sub Chinaco Blanco!" That means we're out of one thing and we are therefore using a substitute (comparable in price and taste) for all cocktails that call for the previous ingredient. (This also applies to food.)

VODKA:
The OG Spirit

Vodka always reminds us of some kind of beginning. It's clear, it's crisp, and it's a classic. In the bar's well, it is the first in line, followed by gin, rum, tequila, bourbon, and rye. It takes the number-one spot for a very good reason: it is the most commonly ordered spirit, and needs to be close to the bartender at all times. Believe us, when you're seven drink tickets deep on a Saturday night, you want that within arm's distance.

Vodka wasn't always the most popular spirit in America. In fact, it was relatively unknown in this country until the 1950s and didn't really take off until the 1970s. For better or worse, a lot of vodka's success can be attributed to excellent marketing campaigns and pop culture. When we think of James Bond swirling his vodka martini, or Carrie Bradshaw and company sipping Cosmos, we think of luxury, mystery, and class. It also doesn't hurt that vodka is virtually odorless and flavorless. It's a good choice for people who simply don't like the taste of alcohol but still want to imbibe.

Vodka is distilled from grain, sugar beets, or sometimes potatoes. Simple as that. Distillers will first choose a starch and add water so that the starch converts to sugar. They then add yeast, which converts the sugar into alcohol (a process known as fermentation). The result is basically a beer, but it's not a beer we'd want to drink, thank you. The "beer" is then run through a still, which separates the alcohol from the water and other compounds by heating the "beer" to different boiling points. Alcohol boils faster than water, which turns it to steam that is then separated out and left to condense, leaving the water behind. It's at once both simple and scientific. All sprits are made in the same way. A beer or wine-like product is fermented and then distilled to pull out more of the alcohol in it.

BAR BANTER

Vodka comes from the Russian word for "water": *voda*. Similarly, *whiskey* comes from the Gaelic word for "water." Sensing a trend? It goes without saying that despite the names' origins, these spirits will not hydrate you.

GIN:

The Gateway Alcohol

We have a friend who bartends at a farm-to-table restaurant. When someone asks if he has any flavored vodka, he responds with "I have gin." That's funny and condescending, but it is a fair description of gin. Gin is very similar to vodka at its core; it's still a grain alcohol, but its biggest and most important difference is juniper. The mash bill must be at least 70% juniper.

In fact, we have even tasted a "flavored vodka" that was meant to be a gin, with all the right botanicals but not enough juniper. The cool thing about gin is how unique each one is, based on the flora and overall local terroir that affect the flavors of different gins. These differences make gin a great spirit to stir or shake with.

BAR BANTER

We like to think of gin as "the gateway alcohol" to whiskey. It's a step up from vodka (a big step), and as we said before, it changes a lot depending on where it was made and its mash bill. Sound familiar? Heck, you can even get barrel-aged gin, which is darker and has a lot of the same vanilla and caramel flavors you'd normally associate with whiskey!

RUM:

The Chameleon of the Cocktail World

Rum is like *The First Wives Club*: it's the unappreciated old-timey spirit. Nowadays, whiskey is getting a lot of attention. It's an ancient spirit and it takes time to craft and age (and that's amazing in its own right), but it's important to appreciate rum for its age and craft as well. By knowing where it comes from, you can better appreciate what you're drinking.

The cool thing about rum is that, much like second wives, it's cheap! Kidding! What we really mean is that it's less expensive to make than a spirit like whiskey. It doesn't need to be aged for many years and it doesn't create a lot of waste. Whiskey, tequila, and mezcal all make a lot of waste. *So* much waste, like more waste than a power plant Captain Planet would take down.

Rum is made from molasses, fresh sugar cane juice (yum), and/or evaporated cane sugar. Most of the rums you encounter (unless you live in the tropics) are made from molasses and evaporated cane sugar. The reason most rum is made from evaporated cane sugar instead of the fresh cane juice is because, like all good things, fresh cane juice spoils quickly. It is really only used in rum-making in places like Guadeloupe, Haiti, and Martinique.

BARTENDER SAYS

"Rum is the Wild West of spirits. No law in any country has any meaningful standards about how rum should be distilled or the ingredients that go into it. Even the rums that aren't 'flavored' still have no rules that say that you can't add flavors."

—*Colin Kiley, Bartender at Puritan & Company, Cambridge, MA*

PRO TIP

Navy Strength Rum was a term coined by the British Royal Navy. They wanted to ensure that if the rum on board one of their ships spilled, It wouldn't prevent their gunpowder from igniting. Therefore, all the rum on board their ships had to be high proof and extremely flammable.

Don't get Navy Strength Rum confused with Navy Rum. Navy Rum also came from the British Royal Navy, but rather than being flammable, Navy Rum was the term for the rum portions given to the sailors.

BAR BANTER

Tiki-style cocktails predominantly involve rum. They are usually mixed with citrus, pineapple, and/or cinnamon and spice flavors. Rum and tiki culture hit America in the 1930s, but even more so when the WWII soldiers began coming home in the 1940s. Soldiers typically trained in environments that were most similar to where they'd be fighting on the front lines, so when they were planning to invade Japan, thousands of American soldiers trained in tropical climates, such as the Philippines, as they prepared for the Pacific Theatre. Needless to say, those boys got a taste of rum and tiki drinks during their time overseas and brought those recipes and tastes home with them.

TEQUILA:
Temptress of the Spirit World

Let's talk about the capricious temptress of the spirit world, the one that almost everyone has a story about. That devilish trickster that many of us can't turn away from, and more of us wish we had.

Tequila.

Tequila is a spirit produced in Mexico and derived from the agave plant. In order for a spirit to be legally classified tequila, it must be made from the Tequilana Weber Blue species of agave. There are a number of subclassifications of tequila, which means there are some decisions to be made. We're here on the front lines to make sure you're making the right decisions: the decisions that will lead to a successful evening that doesn't end facedown in porcelain (we've all been there).

BAR BANTER

Tequila can be broken down into two main categories: 100% agave and mixto. As the name indicates, 100% agave is made only from blue agave. Mixto tequila can be made from at least 51% agave and up to 49% added sugars, usually hangover-inducing cane sugar. If you want to avoid hugging your toilet bowl, repeat after us: "I will not drink mixto tequila."

BAR LINGO

Margarita Glass: There are many origin stories regarding the half-flute, half-coupe "Margarita glass." The stories are more than speculation. The most likely explanation is that they were created around the time that frozen Margaritas became popular. Their wide shape allows for plenty of slushy frozen tequila goodness without washing all of the salt off the rim.

"Training Wheels": This is what we call the lime wedge and salt that are ordered with a shot of tequila. If you need those to do a shot of tequila, the tequila is probably poor quality or you can't handle doing a shot. Remember, good alcohol means it tastes good too. And call us old-fashioned, but if you can't do a shot without training wheels, can you really do a shot? ▸

"Skinny Girl Margarita": That's not a thing. Unless you're talking about the brand of bottled product, which isn't something you're likely to find in a bar. If you want a Margarita but want to skimp on the calories, ask for a Tequila Gimlet that's very light on the simple syrup (or sub agave if it's available).

Frozen vs. On the Rocks: Pretty straightforward. Frozen drinks come from slush machines and/or blenders. Rocks is just ice. Be careful with frozen Margaritas and be aware of your surroundings. If you're on the Jersey Shore with Snooki in 2009, walk away, loser. But also know that ordering a frozen Margarita is ordering something that is probably processed sugar and regrets. If you're at a small, craft cocktail bar, that frozen Margarita was probably made this morning with fresh citrus. Never be afraid to ask either way!

MEZCAL

Most often the term *mezcal* is used to refer to the spirit made primarily in Oaxaca from the espadin species of agave, which has a smoky quality from the slow baking of the agave piña in clay ovens over hot rocks. Mezcal is the general category of which tequila is a subcategory. It is the name given to the distillate made from any type of Mexican agave, not just blue agave.

It's a little confusing. Let us break it down: all tequila is mezcal, but not all mezcal is tequila.

Way, way, way back in the olden times when we started bartending, mezcal wasn't just "new" to American bars, it was "gross" to most American drinkers. We once had a beautiful cocktail on our menu with mezcal, pineapple, a touch of Fernet-Branca (an amaro), among other glorious fresh ingredients. Customers sent it back *constantly*. Not because it had a bad flavor profile, but because people didn't know what the "the Band-Aid taste" was in their drink. Basically, they didn't know what mezcal was or what it would taste like.

You kids are fortunate that you do not live in those times. Nowadays, bartenders and daywalkers alike embrace mezcal. They know that it isn't going to taste like silver tequila and they embrace what it brings to their sick-of-everything-else-palates.

PRO TIP

We can't talk about mezcal without giving a nod to the Del Maguey line. They brought mezcal to the forefront, and these days you can't go anywhere without seeing one of those beautiful green bottles full of beautiful clear liquid. Their Vida and Chichicapa are magnificent. Some of our other favorites include Fidencio Pechuga, Xicaru, and Ilegal Reposado.

AMERICAN WHISKEYS:
a.k.a. 95% of the Whiskey You Will Encounter in a Bar

Just like the word *wine*, *whiskey* is a category of liquor with various subcategories. You wouldn't go to a bar and order "a wine, please," and you wouldn't order "a whiskey" either. Well, you could just order a whiskey, but the bartenders would probably make fun of you behind your back. Instead, you would ask for a specific style and make.

When it comes to whiskey, you have Scotch and Irish, Canadian, Japanese, and then bourbon and rye, the American whiskey sisters. If you know nothing else about whiskey, know that the difference between bourbon and rye is that bourbon tends to be sweeter and must be both 51% or more corn and aged in virgin oak barrels for at least 2 years. Rye is a bit spicier and must be 51% or more rye. Basically, even though it's older, bourbon is like rye's sweet little sister. So if you like your drinks to be a touch on the sweeter side, go for the bourbon. If you like a little spice, stick to rye.

BAR BANTER

It's a common practice to rotate barrels in order to optimize the amount of wood the bourbon touches while it's aging. Tuthilltown Spirits in New York wanted to figure out a good way to expedite this process. Eventually, they put speakers throughout their warehouses and turned loud music with a heavy bass line all the way up. The movement created by the loud music makes the whiskey inside the barrels rock, so more whiskey comes into contact with the barrels. Their bourbon has literally been rocked into existence by various genres of music, like a beautiful little baby. It is appropriately called Hudson Baby Bourbon, because the whiskey has been "rocked" to sleep.

Another aging practice some are now trying is aging whiskey at sea. The Kentucky Artisan Distillery did this for their Jefferson's Ocean release. This process is done to optimize the amount of time the bourbon gets in the barrels (because of the constant rocking motion), but it also exposes the barrels to sea air, which is quite different than the humid air you get on land. It's a delicious experiment, and we recommend trying a bottle if you see it!

SCOTCH

Ah, Scotch. The beginning of whiskey. The word itself is Celtic and has traditionally indicated that the spirit comes from Scotland or Ireland. (Of course that changed with the birth of American, Canadian, and now Japanese whiskeys.)

Scotch isn't for everyone and we find that when it comes to "stubborn drinkers," Scotch and vodka drinkers are typically the most married to their brands. We think that makes more sense for Scotch drinkers, as Scotches are so unique to where they're from and how they're made. (Vodka drinkers: get over it; not everyone is going to carry Grey Goose.)

Scotch, like all whiskeys, has a common association with old men smoking cigars. But guess what? There are not, nor should there be, any gender norms associated with Scotch or any other spirit. We've said it before and we'll say it again: drink if you like it—that's the only rule.

Scotch can be enjoyed neat, on the rocks, or in a cocktail. If you're mixing or sipping it, the same rules apply as with any other spirit. Those rules are: remember to be kind to your wallet when ordering a shaken cocktail or highball, splurge on something you're sipping on whether it's on the rocks or neat, and use your judgment with stirred cocktails. A Manhattan or Rob Roy make sense with higher-end whiskey, but something with a strong flavor like Campari will probably overpower the intricate flavors of a high-end Scotch. If that's the case, is it really worth the price tag? The correct answer is no.

ROOTS MATTER

There are four types of Scotch, which are categorized by where they are distilled. The four styles are: Lowlands, Speyside, Islay, and Highlands. In order to be considered Scotch, remember that the whiskey must also be aged at least 3 years.

The Lowlands are one of the larger regions but, strangely enough, have very few contemporary distilleries. The region is in the South of Scotland, flatter than the rest of the country and the lowest in elevation. Lowland Scotches tend to be softer, malty, and grassy in taste. Two distilleries that have survived time are Glenkinchie and Auchentoshan. Newcomers have hit the scene as recently as 2003, but all in all, at any given point, there are about four producing distilleries in the entire region.

Despite being one of the smallest regions, Speyside houses almost half of the distilleries in Scotland. It's in the northeast of the country and includes the coast. Speyside Scotches tend to be sweet, mellow, and fruity. Our favorite Speyside Scotches are Macallan and Balvenie.

Highland includes the Islands and is the largest region, therefore it has the largest variation of Scotches because of its vast size. The terrain tends to be more rugged. Our favorite Highlands are Oban and Highland Park.

Islay (eye-lah) is a tiny island home to eight working distilleries. This is the strongest flavor identity in all four of the regions due to the malted barely being dried over peat smoke. Our favorites are Lagavulin (also one of our dream distilleries to visit) and Laphroaig.

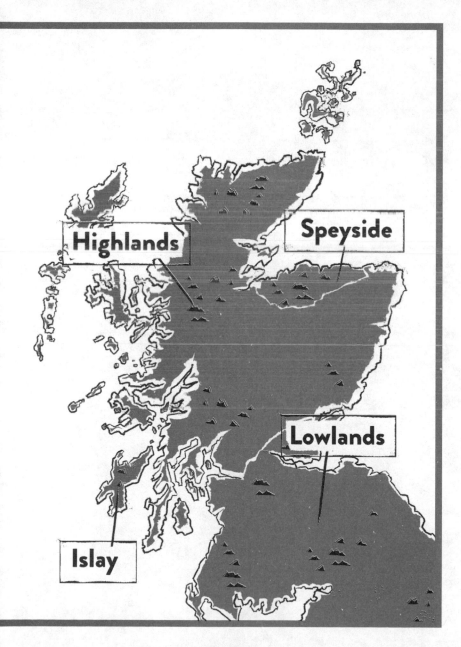

Highlands

Speyside

Islay

Lowlands

BARTENDER SAYS

"Scotch really is the purest reflection
of the terroir surrounding where
it was distilled."

—*Paulo Pereira, General Manager and
Beverage Director at Brass Union, Somerville, MA*

BAR BANTER

Legend has it that the thirteenth-century scholar Michael Scot invented Scotch. Scot was an astrologer, "wizard," and alchemist of the Holy Roman Empire. (He was a bit of a celebrity and even appears in Dante's *Inferno*!) Though Scotch's origin can't be attributed solely to one person, Scot gets mad cred in lure and ballads.

IRISH WHISKEY

Just like Scotch, Irish whiskey is an OG. They are the mother and father of American, Canadian, and Japanese whiskeys, and just like the Beastie Boys, even if they're not your cup of tea, they deserve your respect. Irish whiskey is a triple-distilled blend of pot-stilled malt whiskey, pot-stilled unmalted barley whiskey, and/or column-stilled grain whiskey. After distillation, Irish whiskey is usually aged in old American whiskey or Spanish sherry casks.

There are many different styles in which Irish whiskey can be made. To make it an Irish whiskey, it must be made in a little country called Ireland.

CANADIAN WHISKEY:
The Sangria of Whiskey

That's right—Canadian whiskey is the sangria of whiskey. That means snobs like us don't drink it. Just kidding. But seriously, Canadian whiskeys are blends, and we tend to prefer them for mixing rather than sipping. Canadian whiskeys are usually made with a rye that is blended with a neutral spirit. They must be aged, like bourbon, but for at least 3 years, and it doesn't matter whether or not the barrels are virgin.

JAPANESE WHISKEY

Japanese whiskey is comparatively new (it has only been produced for roughly 75 years), but it has gained popularity in America during the last several years. Japanese whiskey is largely inspired by Scotch, and distilleries often even import peat and barley from Scotland for production. The whiskey is triple-distilled and aged in Japanese oak as well as American and Spanish oak barrels. Simply put: Japanese whiskey must be distilled in Japan in order to be categorized as such. Otherwise, mash bill, aging, and other formal regulations do not (yet) exist.

BAR BANTER

Yet another cool story about the word *whiskey* is its possible origin in Ireland. Legend has it, when Roman or Norman explorers came to Ireland, they discovered what they called "aqua vitae" or "water of life," which was a grape distillate. In Irish Celtic, the words translate to "uisce beatha." When the English invaders from Henry II came to Ireland, they mispronounced and shortened the words to "ushky," which eventually became "whiskey."

BEER:

The Golden Retriever of Alcohol
(Loyal, Fun, and Always Around)

Oh man, where do we even begin? Beer is one of our favorite subjects. In fact, it's what brought us together in the first place. We met in 2009 at a craft beer bar in Somerville, Massachusetts, that had 32 rotating draft lines and over 60 different kinds of bottled beer. We were in our early twenties and tasting beers that most people twice as old as us had never heard of—we were right there in the thick of the emergence of American craft beer. Ah, to be young.

It's been said that beer is the oldest alcoholic beverage (not by us, we never said that, but it's true). From the Trappist beers brewed in Belgium to golden lagers crafted in the U.S.A., there are so many styles of beer, it's hard to keep them straight.

Don't worry. We've got your back. To start, remember that even though there are tons and tons of different kinds of beer, they all stem from two styles of brewing: ales or lagers. They are the roots of the beer tree; everything else branches off from there.

TIME TO GET TECHNICAL!

There are four basic elements included in every single beer: hops, yeast, water, and grain. In fact, for quality control, some countries, like Germany, even have laws in place to ensure that breweries are *only* allowed to use the four elements. Here's what you need to know:

Hops: The flowers of the hop plant—a climbing vine of which there are many varieties. Hops give beer that "bitter" bite. Nowadays, many pale ales and IPAs note exactly which hops are used, or predominately used, in the beer.

Yeast: Little microorganisms that kick-start the fermentation process by chowing down on sugar and farting out the alcohol and carbonation. Seriously, that's an accurate breakdown. Why do you think beer makes you burp? (Just kidding...it's not related.)

Water: Just like humans, beer is mostly water! No wonder we get along so well!

Grain: Usually this takes the form of malted barley, but some brewers, especially homebrewers, prefer to use liquid malt extract. All kinds of grain can be used. This is what differentiates your wheat beers from your oatmeal stouts or corn lagers.

BAR LINGO

The following are a few terms you may see on your beer menu:

Dry-Hopped: The hops are added toward the end of the brewing process. This adds lots of floral hop aroma without a ton of bitterness.

Wet-Hopped: This refers to freshly harvested hops that are used immediately (within 24–48 hours of harvest) without being dried first. (Fun fact: a wet hop can be used as a dry hop if it's added at the end of the brewing process!)

Cask Conditioned: Unfiltered beer that finishes fermenting and carbonating in casks stored in cool cellars.

Nitro: Nitrogen is added to give beer a silky texture and creamy mouthfeel. This is how Guinness gets its awesome texture.

TYPES OF BEER

Beers are like people: unique and difficult to categorize. First, it's helpful to note that ales and lagers are the foundation to many beers, as you can see in this handy chart.

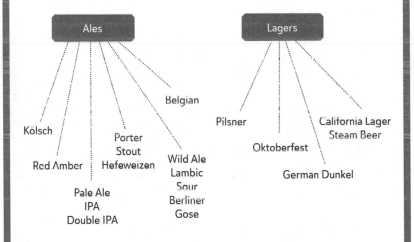

Now, we don't like to put beer into boxes any more than we like to put humans into boxes, but this is a book, so we did it anyway. In the end, we decided to compare our beers to our love lives. That's normal, right?

We like our beer like we like our men.

DELICATE

Lager: Lagers are lighter beers with crisp and sometimes slightly hoppy tastes. They're excellent for hot summer days. Lagers are bottom-fermented, which makes their flavor depend very largely on the yeast strain used to brew. They're one of our go-to refreshing beers because they're simple and so easy to drink.

Kölsch: The Kölsch! This has to be one of our favorite beers. For a beer to be a Kölsch, it must come from Cologne, Germany. It is super light and crisp, much like a Pilsner. The Reissdorf Kölsch steals the show for us.

Hefeweizen: Hefeweizen is a super popular style of beer. It's wheaty, malty, and sweet. This is that beer you see in the tall hourglass-shaped glasses (actually called a Weizen glass) with a super thick head.

THE ONES WHO DON'T GIVE A DAMN ABOUT TITLES

Ales: Ales are top-fermented, which makes the beer ferment faster and be less dependent on the flavor strain. Top-fermenting creates thick, rich yeast heads on the beer. It's crazy to think that the two distinct styles of ales and lagers are created by just the temperature of the room they are fermented in, but it's true. Ales are going to be far less crisp, more full-bodied, and even darker in color than lagers. You'll see ales ranging from the palest blonde to pitch black.

Belgian: This is a huge category! To be a Belgian beer means, first, to be made in Belgium. (Notice a pattern?) Belgian beer is an ale, so it ferments faster and gets that rich yeasty head. It is unique in the variety of flavors elicited from the hops and malts used in distilling. Belgians are going to be fruity and herbal, will sometimes even taste like clove or bubblegum, and are available in a range of styles and colors.

Red Beer: Yet another huge category! You should be able to figure out a distinguishing characteristic of these beers (unless you're like most of Thea's family: color blind). They're also sweet, fruity, and far more malty than hoppy.

BITTER

Pale Ales: A lighter colored ale made with pale malt. Pale ales can lean hop heavy or malt heavy, depending on the brewer, and are a great choice when you want something in the middle. They've got enough weight to them that you won't feel like you're drinking water, but they're not so strong or heavy that you can't have more than one.

IPAs: India pale ales are packed with hops, which gives them the piney, citrusy, tropical, and—yes—often quite bitter flavors. IPAs are popular among homebrewers because the bitter hoppiness masks any mistakes and off flavors that might be present in the beer.

Double/Triple IPAs: A double IPA, a.k.a. an Imperial IPA, is like an IPA with one of those Snapchat filters the kids are using. What we mean to say (well, Thea does; Lauren doesn't know how to use technology) is that an Imperial IPA is an IPA, but more extreme. All those bitter notes—everything you love about an IPA—are amplified in an Imperial. A triple IPA is even more bitter and higher in ABV (alcohol by volume) than an Imperial or an IPA. The alcohol content is also amplified in these beers, and be forewarned, some of them tend to have a pretty intense malty/sweet backbone behind all of those hops. In order to pump up the ABV, brewers need to add more sugar for the yeast to convert to alcohol.

HOLIER THAN THOU

Abbey Ales: These beers get their name because they were brewed by Belgian monks in (you guessed it) abbeys. Not all abbey ales nowadays are. This is a huge category and we couldn't possibly go into serious depth about abbey ales, so for now let us just say that it refers to all beers brewed in abbeys by Trappist monks and beers brewed in the image of the monks' abbey ale style.

Trappist Ales: To be considered a Trappist ale, the beer must be brewed inside a Trappist brewery. Trappist monks are known for vows of silence and charitable work. They are a subset of Cistercian monks, with a history tracing back as far as 1664. These monks, like so many before and after, made alcohol, and by God they did it well. Today, most Trappist breweries are in Belgium, but there are several in the Netherlands and even one in the good ol' U.S. of A. Spencer Trappist Brewery in Spencer, Massachusetts, produces the world's first American Trappist Ale, made by actual Trappist monks. They devote their time to making jams and beer and, of course, focus largely on charitable work. In case you want to be just like us, our favorite Trappists are Brasserie d'Orval and Bières de Chimay.

SOUR

Sours are so hot right now. And they're hot because they're awesome. We *love* sours. (But we loved them before they were cool, just sayin'.) We love Goses, we love lambics, we love Berliners, and we love wild ales. We highly recommend trying all of them when you get a chance. They are all unique and beautiful snowflakes of the beer world.

Berliner: Just like a Kölsch, in order to be called a Berliner, the beer must be from (you guessed it) Germany. Berliners are ales and are traditionally lower in alcohol. They are light, tart, and inexpensive. Their tartness is cut in Europe with an assortment of fruit-flavored syrups you can add to your taste. Of course, in America, it must be called a Berliner-style, and many breweries have started taking it upon themselves to add the fruit during the distillation process. White Birch Brewing in Hookset, New Hampshire, puts out a beautiful Berliner Weisse year-round that is good with or without syrup.

Gose: Like so many beautiful beers, Gose (pronounced "go-sah") is a style of sour that originated in Goslar, Germany. Its signature notes are citrus, herbs, and most of all: salt. Goses definitely aren't for everyone, and you may not like them the first time you try them. They grow on you once you know what to expect, and we think they're the most refreshing style of beer to drink when it's hot out and you're thirsty. One of our favorites is the Two Evil Geyser Gose, a collaboration between Evil Twin Brewing in Brooklyn, New York, and Two Roads Brewing in Stratford, Connecticut.

Wild Ales: Wild ales are beers that are brewed with wild yeast, such as Brettanomyces (or "Brett"). They're funky, tart, and rustic (just like our all-girl country soul band).

Lambics: We'd write an ode to lambics if we could. We'd write sonnets, we'd build altars—you get the picture. Lambics are spontaneously fermented, unblended ales that are made in Belgium. Lambics are extremely tart because they are brewed with wild yeast and allowed to ferment with naturally occurring bacteria and then aged in barrels. The best of the best come from Brasserie Cantillon in Brussels. If you see this name anywhere, buy it (and buy a second one for us!).

Flanders: Another tart delicious treat from Belgium. These are extremely tart and ever so slightly vinegary. If you love balsamic vinegar or kombucha, this is the style for you. They are distinctive in their long-term aging in barrels and because they are often a blend of newer and older beers. If you ever see the Duchesse de Bourgogne, don't let her walk by.

COMPLEX AND MOODY

Porter: Porters are dark, rich, and roasted. They are made from brown malted barley and originated in England.

Stouts: Little sisters to porters, stouts are dark beers made with roasted malted and unmalted barley. The most famous stout is probably Guinness (have you heard of it?). These beers are thick, rich, and chewy.

Cider: Cider is made by fermenting the juice of apples. Styles range from the sweet golden yellow concoctions, harsh "Scrumpy," or refreshing low-ABV ciders of the United Kingdom, to funky, effervescent wine-like ciders of northern France and single-apple heirloom varietals or dry-hopped thirst quenchers of the American craft world.

BARTENDER SAYS

"The craft beer scene is an exciting, weird, and wild place right now. As a restaurant buyer with room for 32 draft lines and up to 40 bottles and cans, I still find myself never being able to quite satisfy everyone's needs. It is a challenge to balance styles, popular brands, produce big events that feature one or more brewery, take care of the brewery startup down the street, take care of the rep who helps you out the most, and meet budget costs. That's just the behind the scenes. Every day I ask my staff what brands or styles of beer are people asking for. One day it's black IPAs, the next it's red ales, then sours, then Goses, then fruit beers. The list is endless."

—Geoffrey Thompson, Beer Czar at Foundry on Elm and Saloon, Somerville, MA

WINE:

The Pretentious Older Sibling You're Always Trying to Live Up To

Talking about, and ordering, wine can be at once intimidating and divisive. You're either trashy or you're a wine snob—there's no winning. We think wine should be fun, and everyone should feel free to swirl or chug to their heart's content.

No one knows everything, which means that no one expects you to know everything either! When ordering wine, feel free to ask for specific tastes, but also remember this important thing: *read the menu*. Don't ask for a taste of a wine that is only sold by the bottle. Don't ask for the Pinot Noir without looking to see if the bar even has a Pinot Noir. Instead, ask: "I see you don't have a Pinot Noir, what would you recommend instead?" See how easy that is?

PRO TIP

There are over 1,300 different grape varietals, so don't be hard on yourself when you come across one you've never heard of! Also, please consider that along with those varietals there are different regions, so you could have the same grape from different regions and totally just blow your socks off by tasting them next to each other. This is how we have fun—is that normal? Guys?

GRAPE MYSTERY

The same grapes grown in different regions and under different conditions will produce very different tasting wines, but here are some common flavors you might find in some of the wines you probably encounter the most often:

- ▶ **Grüner Veltliner:** Green Apple, Herbs, White Pepper
- ▶ **Sauvignon Blanc:** Lime, Melon, Green Pepper
- ▶ **Chardonnay:** Butter, Toffee, Golden Delicious Apple, Peach
- ▶ **Riesling:** Lime, Jasmine, Honeysuckle, Apricot
- ▶ **Rosé:** Strawberry, Pink Grapefruit, Flower Petals, Wet Rocks
- ▶ **Pinot Noir:** Raspberry, Warm Spices, Dirt, Tobacco
- ▶ **Grenache:** Leather, Licorice, Plum
- ▶ **Merlot:** Anise, Cedar, Cherry, Dirt
- ▶ **Cabernet Franc:** Coffee, Chili Pepper, Black Cherry
- ▶ **Cabernet Sauvignon:** Green Pepper, Cherry, Baking Spices
- ▶ **Malbec:** Plum, Chocolate, Dried Fruit
- ▶ **Syrah:** Cooked Fruit, Tobacco, Roasted Meat

ROSÉ

People are into rosé right now, but it is by no means a new style of wine. It is also by no means a wine made with specific grapes. Rosé is made when red grape skins are macerated in grape juice (either red, white, or a combination of both). Rosé is made all over the world and with every varietal of grape.

Just like all other types of alcohol, different kinds of rosés are made in different ways. The most common is dyeing the wine pink by letting it sit for a short period of time (between 2 and 24 hours) with red grape skins. Some are simply blends of red and white wine. One tactic used for making sparkling rosé is to bleed off the immediate red wine juices when making one red wine and separating those juices out to be a rosé. This is called the bleeding or saignée (san-yay) method.

Rosés can be sweet but they can also be super dry. They can be funky or earthy. Every rosé is going to be different, so definitely read the descriptions, Google them, and, of course, ask the bartender!

CHAMPAGNE VS. PROSECCO

Both have bubbles and both are European, so what's the difference?

The first and easiest difference to remember is the regions where they are made. Champagne must be made in the Champagne region of France. Prosecco, on the other hand, must come from the Veneto region of Italy.

Secondly, the grapes used for Champagne are largely Chardonnay, Pinot Noir, and Pinot Meunier, but, just to confuse things, Petit Meslier, Arbane, Pinot Gris, and Pinot Blanc are also used. Prosecco uses Glera grapes. Nice and easy.

Champagne is made using the traditional or classic method while Prosecco is fermented using the less expensive tank method. We won't walk you through each step, but we will tell you that the traditional method has five more steps than the tank method, which helps account for the price difference between Prosecco and Champagne.

PRO TIP

What the heck does "sur lie" mean?
You may come across a bottle of white or
sparkling wine with the words "Sur Lie"
printed on it. Sur lie means that a wine
has been aged "on the lees" (still not
super helpful, but bear with us). "Lees"
are essentially dead yeast particles left
over from the winemaking process.
The wines are aged on lees for anywhere
from several months to several years.
The lees give wines a creamy texture
and toasty and biscuity (dare
we say yeasty?) flavors.

2

HOW TO ORDER

This might sound crazy, but when it comes to ordering, it's really good to know what you like and what you want in that moment. Sounds so simple, right? You'd be surprised.

This is when it's smart and effective to ask questions about different drink ingredients and taste various liquors. This really is the only way to figure out what you like. Of course, over time it will all become easier and you'll be able to pinpoint what flavors you love. Just remember: don't feel bad about asking to try something you've never had before. Your bartender would rather give you a small taste of something and have you hate it than make an entire drink for you and find out later that you weren't happy.

PRO TIP

If a spirit has been distilled many times, it's often a reflection of the quality of starches used to make it. So don't be fooled by a label bragging about a dozen distills. The distiller probably just spent a lot of time and energy trying to mask an inferior product—yuck!

BAR BANTER

Vodka has a reputation for being
"the alcoholic's drink of choice" because it is
colorless and odorless. Don't let that little bit of
info scare you away, though. It's a classic
spirit, without which we would never have
had the pleasure of the Cosmopolitan.
No one wants to imagine a world
without the Cosmo.

ROOKIE MISTAKE

Don't assume that a vodka soda is somehow better for you than any other spirit.
One serving of vodka has the same num
ber of calories as a serving of tequila,
gin, rum, or whiskey. Sure, a vodka soda
has fewer calories than a whiskey and
coke, but that's because you're pairing
whiskey with coke. The main source of
calories in alcohol is...well...alcohol.
Unless you're drinking something low
in alcohol, the calories are all going
to be about the same.

PRO TIP

Instead of turning to flavored vodka, take a minute to identify what you like about your flavored vodka of choice. Is it sweet? Is it savory? Is it lemon, peach, grapefruit? All of those flavors (and many more) can be had as liqueurs made by stellar distilleries with long histories of fresh, local ingredients. Combier, the original producer and creator of orange liqueur, has an enormous liqueur line that is truly excellent. Just like using fresh juice as opposed to something processed, mixing a cocktail with a liqueur like that can make a huge difference in the quality of your drink.

True story: we once had a very confusing conversation with a woman who didn't understand why her blueberry vodka and soda water was blue. We had to explain to her that the vodka had been dyed blue by the blueberries. This shouldn't be confusing, but it is, because so much flavored vodka is infused with chemicals and not real fruit. Gross.

ROOKIE MISTAKE

Rum doesn't always have to be in a shaken drink or a highball. It's really wonderful in a stirred drink too. One of our favorite games to play is to exchange a whiskey in a stirred cocktail with an aged rum instead. Those same warm notes you get in a bourbon are also going to appear in an aged rum. Have fun and don't be self-conscious about making a gross mistake when mixing. You can always start over! This is just one fun thing about rum. It really is versatile and pairs well with many different flavors. If you're overmixing with vodka and are looking for the next challenge, we'd recommend moving on to rum.

BAR LINGO

There are five major types of rum: white rum, spiced rum, aged rum, rhum agricole, and cachaça. You probably are pretty familiar with the first two, may be acquaintances with the third, and are likely a stranger to the fourth and fifth.

White Rum is most likely what comes to mind first when you think of rum, followed closely by spiced rum. It's third in the bar well, so it's very commonly ordered. White rum is usually what people want when they throw their standard "Bacardi and Coke" order at a bartender. White rum isn't as much white as it is clear, but that's just semantics. It's unique because, since it is unaged, it is ready to drink right off the still (what the spirit is distilled in). It's worth noting that some white rum is "rested" in stainless steel casks for anywhere from several months to several years, and some countries require that all rums (even white rum) undergo an aging process.

Spiced Rum is another very common order at the bar. It's very often ordered in a highball format. Believe it or not, people often order spiced rum without realizing it when they send out that request for a "Captain and Coke." Captain Morgan, or its comparable rival, Sailor Jerry, is a spiced rum. This is where rum gets browner in color and you start to notice those cinnamon and warm spice notes. It will heat up your drink with its warm flavors. Believe it or not, the first cocktail to popularize rum in America was actually a Hot Toddy. The nicest (and most expensive!) toddies added spices to the rum and hot water.

Aged Rum is—you guessed it—aged rum. A stint in oak barrels gives the rum a deeper color and warm vanilla, caramel, and spice flavors that are more unique to the aging process. Aged rum has less of that "flavor added" taste than what you may find in spiced rums.

Rhum Agricole (or agriculture rum) is made from fresh cane sugar and is more terroir-driven and vegetal than other rums. It's going to taste grassier, more "rustic," and yes, sometimes harsher or less refined than the other styles.

Cachaça is a special rum only made in Brazil from fresh-cut sugar cane.

Our Favorites: GrandTen Rare Bird Overproof, Old Monk Rum, and La Favorite Rhum Agricole

BAR LINGO

There are three major types of gin: London Dry, Old Tom, and Plymouth. But before we get started on gin, we need to take a minute to talk about Genever.

Genever is otherwise known as junever, jenever, jeniever, peket, or Holland gin. Genever is the mother of gin—its predecessor. Like most spirits and liqueurs, it is believed to have been invented by an alchemist to be used as a medicine. Legend says Sylvius de Bouve created genever way back in the sixteenth century. If you like gin, you will probably like genever. That's because it has very similar tasting notes as gin, but with more grain and cereal notes instead of the herbal botanicals you get from a gin.

Old Tom is the next step in the progression toward gin. It used to be a lot more common behind the bar, but Prohibition went and threw a wrench into that. Fortunately, since the cocktail revival movement kicked in over the past several years, most bars will have at least one Old Tom gin back there. Tasting notes include brown sugar, spices, dried fruit, and vanilla.

London Dry Gin is exactly what it sounds like: dry gin. This gin must come from London, just like a Czech Pilsner must come from the Czech Republic or Reissdorf Kölsch must come from Cologne, Germany. Every other London Dry must have the added word "style" at the end of it. London Dry gins tend to taste juniper heavy, with a touch of citrus.

Plymouth Gin is both a brand and a style of gin. Pretty simple, Plymouth Gin (the flat bottle with a greenish tint) is the only Plymouth Gin. It comes from South West England. It's a touch sweeter and more "rustic" tasting than London Dry.

Hendrick's Gin is a "new" or "international" style gin. It is the only one distilled with rose petals and cucumbers. Yum!

THE MARTINI

Once upon a time, there was a cocktail called the Martinez. It is made with gin, Maraschino liqueur (a liqueur made with Marasca cherries), sweet vermouth, and a dash of Angostura bitters. It is delicious. Just by name alone you can see how we will soon get to the Martini.

The classic Martini was made by doing away with the Maraschino liqueur, swapping the sweet vermouth for dry, and switching out the Angostura for orange bitters. Bam. Nowadays, most people like their Martinis with vodka and very little vermouth. Dirty Martinis are also super popular. It's all about your taste preference.

MARTINEZ

2 oz. gin
¾ oz. sweet vermouth
¼ oz. Maraschino liqueur
Dash Angostura bitters
Lemon twist

Add ingredients (except twist) and ice to a cocktail shaker or mixing glass. Stir and strain into a cocktail or rocks glass. Serve with lemon twist.

Martinez

PRO TIP

HOW TO ORDER A MARTINI IN 2017

Remember that the classic Martini is made with gin, not vodka. If you want vodka, that's okay! Just make sure you start by specifying which you want.

Do you want it with very little vermouth? That's cool; just say you want it "dry." If you want nearly no vermouth, say "bone dry," and if you want no vermouth, just straight up say "no vermouth."

Next, do you want it salty? Make it dirty!
If you like it super savory, say "extra dirty."

If you don't like olives or salt, don't bring them up at all. The recipe doesn't call for any brine unless you say the word "dirty" out loud to your bartender. You can ask for a twist, which will be made with a lemon unless you're a monster and want a grapefruit or something insane like that.

BAR BANTER

Many pre–Prohibition era cocktail recipes call for Old Tom, as it was more common than gin back then. Its flavor profile is lighter and smoother than genever, and usually has sweeter notes. Old Tom is also going to look more like a whiskey in color. It mixes well and is really delicious to sip on too. (Some distilleries do barrel-age their gin, such as Berkshire Mountain Distillers in Sheffield, Massachusetts; they age their annual batch of Ethereal Gin and the result is simply divine.)

ROOKIE MISTAKE

Know what you want before you order it.
The habit to just order without thinking
about what you want seems especially
prevalent among Martini orders. For
example: don't order it dry unless you
know what vermouth tastes like. Do you
know how many times we get Martinis
sent back for being "too wet" when there
is little to no vermouth at all in them?
Too many times!

TEQUILA TYPES

There are four categories of tequila aging. It's a matter of personal preference what you choose to sip versus what you mix into a cocktail, but if you're going to make a Margarita, save your money and don't use the really expensive stuff. As long as you're using 100% agave tequila it's going to taste great.

▶ **Blanco** (or silver) tequila is bottled immediately after distilling, or after resting in stainless steel for up to 60 days. Blanco tequilas are clean and crisp, often with a peppery bite.

▶ **Reposado** tequila is rested in a wooden barrel (usually American or French oak) for 60 days to a year. Sometimes reposado tequila is aged in barrels that once housed whiskey, cognac, and wine so that the spirit will take on some of that character. Reposados take on some color from the barrel. They tend to be lightly golden in color, and semisweet but still spicy.

▶ **Añejo** tequila is aged in oak barrels for between 1 and 3 years. The oak gives the tequila a darker golden color, and smooth rich flavor.

▶ **Extra Añejo** tequila is aged for a minimum of 3 years. These tend to be the smoothest and most complex of the tequilas and are great for sipping.

▶ **"Gold"** tequila is sometimes a mix of 100% agave blanco and 100% agave reposado, but more often than not, is a mixto tequila with caramel color added. Make sure you read the label. Mixto has loads of sugar in it and will give you a hangover.

PRO TIP

We call this segment "How to make friends with tequila without making friends with your bathroom floor." First off, there is no reason to buy high-end tequila to make Margaritas. If you are breaking out the blender, buy well tequila, like Jose Cuervo. If you are planning on sipping at your leisure, then it's time to spend a little more.

Here are a few of our favorites:

Top Shelf: El Luchador 123 Organic, El Tesoro Reposado

Mid-Level: Casamigos Añejo

Well: Lunazul Blanco

BARTENDER SAYS

"When someone asks me for a Long Island Iced Tea, I automatically red flag them as someone I might have to cut off. It's a drink that screams 'I don't care what I'm drinking, I just want to get drunk.'"

—*Stephen Konrads, Bartender at River Bar, Somerville, MA*

PRO TIP

Half the time when someone orders a Margarita, what they actually want is a Tequila Gimlet. A Margarita is actually an orange-flavored cocktail, whereas a Gimlet will give you more of that tart lime bite. So the next time you're out with your best friend and they say they just really want a "refreshing Margarita," order them a Gimlet instead and watch as they fall in love sip after tart sip.

BAR LINGO

When it's your moment to order, don't panic! Here are some ordering tips to stick to:

Whiskey Neat: If you order a whiskey neat, you will get about 2 ounces of whiskey with no ice.

Whiskey On the Rocks: Order whiskey on the rocks and you will get about 2 ounces of whiskey with ice.

Whiskey Down: Your whiskey will be served in a rocks glass, neat or on the rocks. When ordering a cocktail, you can specify up or down.

Some people believe whiskey should only be consumed "neat" so you don't dilute the liquor, but it completely depends on your taste. The ice can open up your drink and give you a totally different experience than ordering it "neat." If you do order on the rocks, pay attention to the number of ice cubes that are added. There really shouldn't be more than 1 or 2, so specify how many you want.

Rye Favorites: Journeyman 100%, Hudson, Sazerac, Templeton, and Bulleit

Bourbon Favorites: Buffalo Trace, Rowan's Creek, Prichard's Double Barreled, and Blanton's

BAR LINGO

Whisky: The OG spelling. Scotch, Canadian, and the oh-so-hot-right-now Japanese whiskey will probably not have an "e."

Whiskey: Americanized spelling. American and Irish whiskey will probably throw that "e" in there. We'll use this spelling throughout the book to avoid confusion.

Mash Bill: The recipe used to make the whiskey. All bourbons, for example, will always have a mash bill of at least 51% corn.

Single Barrel: Pretty literal, this whiskey was aged in only one barrel. Often, distillers will marry barrels (combine several barrels, a.k.a. blend them) during the bottling process.

Shot: About half an ounce less liquor than if you're ordering it "neat." Served in those famous shooter shot glasses.

Rocks Glass (Old Fashioned Glass): If you order a whiskey neat or on the rocks, it will be served in this. It's down, as opposed to up. Don't worry about this too much—only a cocktail would need to be specified as up or down.

Double Old Fashioned Glass: Wait, what? Yeah, you heard us. This is a larger version of the Old Fashioned or rocks glass. We like them for a well-shaken drink, or a drink on crushed ice (because the crushed ice melts faster and dilutes the drink faster than big ol' cubes—it's called science, people!).

PRO TIP

Be kind to your wallet: you should only upgrade to a better whiskey if you're ordering it neat, on the rocks, or in a stirred cocktail. Once a strong ingredient like, say, ginger beer, citrus, or Coke is in the mix, get that bottom-shelf well whiskey (as long as it doesn't come in a plastic bottle). You won't be able to taste the difference, but your bank account will!

FROM THE TOP ON DOWN

Whiskeys to try, from top shelf down to the well:

Top: Pappy Van Winkle, Lock Stock & Barrel, Prichard's (though rumor has it that the latest Prichard has 86'd whiskey from the distillery; let us pray this isn't true)

Middle: Willett, Blanton's, Rowan's Creek, Journeyman, Bulleit, Buffalo Trace, Maker's Mark

Bottom: Four Roses, Jim Beam, Rittenhouse

BAR BANTER

Lock Stock & Barrel, one of our favorite ryes,
is technically a Canadian whiskey.
Robert J. Cooper, the now-deceased owner of
St-Germain, bought barrels and barrels of
Canadian whiskey before his passing and aged
them all in American oak barrels. He then
resold the product as aged rye with a mash bill
of mostly rye rather than Canadian whiskey.
That is why Lock Stock & Barrel is becoming
harder and harder to get. What we have now is
the last that the world will ever know of it.

PRO TIP

Scotch flavors tend to be woody, earthy, peaty, and smoky. When you're at home trying to mix together something with whatever the hell you have in your fridge—we don't get to "grocery" stores often, guys—take a step back and consider this: if you were cooking, what would you pair with something smoky, like say, barbecue? Even if you don't cook, you can comb your memory and think about what you see on plates at restaurants. Barbecued meat is generally paired with lemon, ginger, maple syrup, etc. Perhaps you have items in your home that have those same flavors. You do? We're so proud!

BAR BANTER

Even though it is made with malted barley, Irish whiskey is not dried over peat, which is why it does not have the peaty notes that you associate with Scotch. This detail is a side effect of just how old Irish whiskey is. Peat-cutting was not mechanized when Irish whiskey was born, and therefore, wood and coal were more plentiful and used to dry the barley. Hence the total lack of peat flavors in Irish whiskey and the lack of similarities in tasting notes between Irish whiskey and Scotch.

BAR LINGO

A **"back"** refers to a small serving of a nonalcoholic beverage that's served in a separate glass alongside an alcoholic
drink, usually a shot or a straight spirit neat or on the rocks.
For example: if you were to ask for "a bourbon neat with a
Coke back" you would get two ounces of bourbon in a rocks
glass with no ice and a few ounces of Coke alongside it in
a separate glass. You won't dilute or change the flavor of
the bourbon at all, but you'll have something to chase the
whiskey with or break up the heat from the alcohol.

A **"pickle back"** refers to a shot of whiskey (usually
Jameson) with a chaser shot of pickle brine. Don't knock
it until you've tried it. And then maybe knock it. To each
their own.

BARTENDER SAYS

"I'm not sure where the impulse to order [dirty rocks on the side] comes from. I've paid close attention to the guests that do and the majority of them seem to add the ice in, bit by bit over time, maybe to cool the drink down? I get the impulse, especially if you drink your Martini slowly, but you're diluting the drink just as much as if it was on the rocks. The other theory is that they got in the habit of going to places where bartenders don't measure their pours and have extra in the shaker after they fill the glass. So therefore, this request can annoy me because it can unintentionally signal two things: 1. That I'm not good and precise at my job. 2. That you're smarter than me and you're going to game me out of that extra liquor."

—*Colin Kiley, Bartender at Puritan & Company, Cambridge, MA*

BAR LINGO

Top-Fermented: Beers that are fermented at higher temperatures (usually between 50°F and 80°F), causing the yeast to rise to the top. It's a process used for a variety of styles, including, but not limited to, ales like Goses, wheats, Kölsches, and porters.

Bottom-Fermented: In these beers, the yeast is fermented at a lower temperature ranging between 45°F and 60°F. The yeast sticks to the bottom and ferments far slower than in top-fermented beers. The flavor of the beer changes drastically depending on the strain of yeast. Some bottom-fermented beers are most famously lagers like Pilsners, Märzens, and Bocks.

Spontaneously Fermented: This beer is fermented uncovered, so it is exposed to the open air around it. Because of this, it's open to the bacteria and natural yeasts in the air that infect the beer. The process creates a tart, funky, and unique flavor. The flavor is enormously affected by the surrounding environment.

Session Beer: This is a term you're going to see a lot nowadays. Some breweries, like Notch Brewery in Salem, Massachusetts, make session beers exclusively. When you see the word *session* you can know one thing for sure: it's going to be low in ABV (alcohol by volume), usually less than 5%.

PRO TIP

Here's a helpful trick: many bars tend to lay out their beers from lighter to darker on their menu. If you know you like dark beers, skip to the end, and you'll see the stouts and porters. If you generally like hoppy beers, take a look at the middle. And obviously, lighter beers are up front. Duh.

BAR BANTER

India pale ales get their name from the
East India Company. The local brewer for the
East India Company added a ridiculous amount
of hops to his beer in order to preserve it for
the lengthy trips across oceans and seas, so
that the merchants would have something
refreshing to drink once they reached the
hot and humid East Indies. The result was
something more than beer—it was a
delicious revolution!

PRO TIP

Most of the calories in beer come from
alcohol, so if you're trying to go
low-calorie but can't stomach the
thought of yet another "light" beer,
go for a session beer, and remember:
Guinness has the same amount
of calories as most light beers.

PRO TIP

A Pilsner is only a Pilsner because it is brewed in Pilsen, Czech Republic. It is a type of lager. We love the Pilsner Urquell for a traditional Czech Pils, but Massachusetts brewery Notch makes a session Czech-style Pils, aptly named Notch Session Pils, that slays.

BAR BANTER

There is a theory that the term "session beer" stems from British pub culture, where bar patrons would sit and enjoy more than a few beers over a long period, or a session. Lower ABV beers make that possible without sloppy (and dangerous!) consequences. In fact, session beers are our favorite choice for day drinking.

Another theory regarding the origins of the session beer comes from World War I England, when laws only allowed workers to have beer twice a day between certain hours. The first drinking session was allowed between 11 a.m. and 3 p.m., so people had to make sure they had a drink or two that wouldn't get them sloshed—they had to go back to work, after all! Therefore, they chose beers that were lower in alcohol. Sidebar: Can you imagine only being able to drink between certain hours of the day? Perish the thought!

BAR BANTER

In Germany, where the drinking age is 16, Hefeweizens are very popular among new and old drinkers alike. Because Hefeweizens are sweet, they are perfect for those just making the transition from nonalcoholic to alcoholic beverages. Still, though, they're not quite sweet enough for some. In Germany, you will see many teenagers drinking "Cola-Weizens," which is half Hefeweizen, half-Coca-Cola. Yes, we've tried it, and it's not awful...

WINE 101:

Grapes vs. Regions

The name of the wine isn't always the grape, it's very often the region. Say what? For example: Burgundy and Bordeaux are regions, not grapes. If you're drinking a white Burgundy, there's a very good chance it's Chardonnay. If it's red, it's very likely a Pinot Noir. Likewise, if you've got a white Bordeaux, there's probably some Sauvignon Blanc in there, and a red Bordeaux is probably some combination of Merlot and Cabernet Sauvignon, possibly with some Cabernet Franc thrown in.

BARTENDER SAYS

"I studied wine so much, I think I learned French!"

—Kelsey Conner, Server at Loyal Nine, Cambridge, MA

WINE FOUND IN EACH FRENCH REGION

LOIRE VALLEY	CHAMPAGNE	ALSACE	BURGUNDY
Sauvignon Blanc	Sparkling Wine	Riesling	Pinot Noir
Muscadet		Pinot Gris	Chardonnay
Chenin Blanc		Gewürztraminer	

BEAUJOLAIS	RHÔNE	CORSE	PROVENCE
Gamay	Syrah	Red and Rosé Blends	Rosé
	Grenache		

LANGUEDOC-ROUSSILLON	SUD-OUEST	BORDEAUX	
Grenache	Malbec	Cabernet Sauvignon	
Carignan		Merlot	
		Sauvignon Blanc	

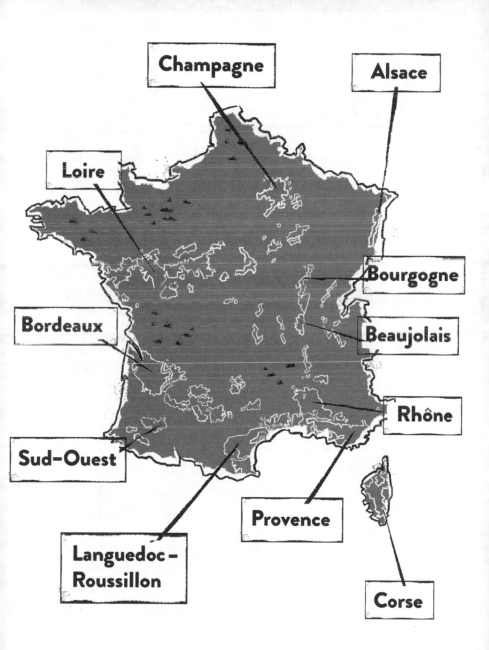

Champagne

Alsace

Loire

Bourgogne

Bordeaux

Beaujolais

Rhône

Sud-Ouest

Provence

Languedoc-
Roussillon

Corse

BAR LINGO

Tannins: Tannins are compounds that occur naturally in a number of plants (including grape skins, seeds, and stems). Tannins have a bitter taste and cause a drying sensation on your tongue. If you've ever peeled the skin off a grape with your teeth or taken a sip of over-steeped black tea you know what we're talking about.

Dry: The opposite of sweet! Plain and simple. When a wine is dry, the winemaker has completely finished the fermentation process, allowing the yeast in the wine to consume all the sugar.

Body: The body of a wine refers to the weight of it on your palate. We like to compare the body of wine to milk. Drinking light-bodied wines feels like drinking water or skim milk, while drinking full-bodied wines is like taking a sip of heavy cream (...yum).

Méthode Champenoise (or Méthode Traditionnelle): The traditional method of sparkling winemaking. Natural carbonation occurs completely inside the bottle.

WINE CHART

If You Like...		Try...
Pinot Grigio	▶	Muscadet, Chenin Blanc
Sauvignon Blanc	▶	Grüner Veltliner, Albariño, Vermentino
Chardonnay	▶	Viognier, Semillon
Riesling	▶	Gewürztraminer, Viognier
Pinot Noir	▶	Cinsault, Carignan, Gamay
Cabernet Sauvignon	▶	Sangiovese, Tempranillo
Merlot	▶	Grenache, Carménère
Malbec	▶	Dolcetto, Nero d'Avola
Shiraz	▶	Syrah (okay, we cheated...it's the same exact grape grown in different regions), Mourvèdre, Malbec (from France)

PRO TIP

If you're choosing wine from a long list
and have no idea where to start, look at
the region that's most represented on
the list. It's probably the region the
wine buyer is most passionate about,
which means any of those are going
to be great wines. For example, if
out of 12 wines on a list, 7 are from
France, there's a good change those
are some of the wine buyer's favorites,
the ones that simply couldn't be
eliminated from the list.

TO OAK OR NOT TO OAK

Many wines spend some amount of time aging in oak barrels. Much as it does with whiskey, the barrel imparts some of its flavor and color to the wine. There are a lot of factors that will determine the way your wine tastes—the terroir of the area in which the grapes are grown, how the wine is made, the varietal of grapes used (duh!), and how much time (if any) the wine spends aging in oak (the alternative being storing it in stainless steel casks). Oak can impart so many different flavors, but here are some of the big ones:

WHITE WINES

- ▶ **Oak:** Vanilla, butter, crème brûlée
- ▶ **No Oak:** Citrus, tropical fruit, honeysuckle, slate

RED WINES

- ▶ **Oak:** Chocolate, caramel, toffee
- ▶ **No Oak:** Fruit, herbs, spices

PRO TIP

If you want a safe way to pick a wine to go with your meal, remember this: things that grow together, go together. If you're dining in an Italian restaurant enjoying some rustic Tuscan cuisine, pick a wine from Tuscany! The grapes grow alongside those same vegetables and herbs that you are about to enjoy (and that your main course, if it's meat, likely ate during its lifetime). It's the most surefire way to ensure you'll be getting complementary flavors.

BARTENDER SAYS

"Embrace the descriptions 'barnyard,' 'cat-piss,' 'gasoline,' 'Band-Aid,' 'wet dog' when describing wine. Though these choice of descriptors may sound unappealing, many times it's expressing the complexity of a good/fun wine."

—*Mika Gagné, Bartender at Saraghina, Brooklyn, NY*

BAR LINGO

USE YOUR WORDS: HOW DO YOU DESCRIBE WHAT YOU'RE DRINKING?

Dry vs. Sweet: As we said before, this one is pretty straightforward, so don't overthink it! If it's sweet it's sweet, but don't mistake sweet for fruity.

Acidic vs. Round: When it comes to acidic wines, it helps to think of biting into a green apple. There's the crisp sound as your teeth sink into the fruit, but there's also that crisp spasm on your tongue from the flavor. That's acidity. It feels like you're immediately salivating out of your tongue. Rounded wines are going to be far less dramatic. It's a silkier, softer, and lush sensation. We like to think of acidic wines as kind of like the end of *Thelma & Louise*. The movie takes you all the way to the edge of that cliff. You've been with them through husbands, abuse, and murder, and then they just drive you right off that edge. Acidic wines drive you off that cliff with them. Rounded wines can take you on an equally dramatic journey, but they're going to make sure you get home safe.

Fruity vs. Earthy: Fruity wines taste like fruit (shocker!), but they don't have to taste exclusively like grapes. All sorts of berry and tree fruit flavors can be present in the wines, despite those fruits never coming in contact with the wine (unless you're making sangria). Earthy wines tend to have more "green" and "brown" flavors found in nature, including, but not limited to, herbal, vegetal, dirt, and yes, even poo flavors. These flavors are all naturally occurring as per the grapes, yeast, terroir, barrels, and aging process.

Juicy vs. Jammy: Juicy tastes like fresh juice (usually grape juice, considering that's what the wine started out as). Jammy wines taste more like sweet (even syrupy) cooked fruit and berries.

ROOKIE MISTAKE

If we don't have the varietal you're
looking for, don't disregard our
suggestions and rattle off other varietals
just because you know their names.
Not every bar can carry every brand or
bottle you're looking for (which is good,
because that would be super boring!).
It's our job to be able to make suggestions and substitutions when they apply.
Trust us, if you're craving a cold glass
of Sauvignon Blanc, a glass of Grüner
Veltliner is going to taste way better
than a glass of Chardonnay.

PRO TIP

Not all Riesling is sweet! There are a lot of wonderful dry Rieslings that have crisp Meyer lemon, lime, and even gingery flavors. In fact, Rieslings are very popular among sommeliers because of their crazy variations. If you are looking for sweet, try a Moscato.

"Though Muscadet may sound like Moscato, don't be confused. *It is not sweet!* In fact, it can be one of the drier white wines out of the Loire Valley you'd be able to find."

—*Mika Gagné, Bartender at Saraghina, Brooklyn, NY*

REMEMBER TO SPEAK UP!

When it comes to cocktails, everyone has their own variation of a classic, per their own taste. Please don't ever be shy about messing with proportions on these classic recipes to make something that you adore.

WHAT SHOULD I DRINK?
I feel like something...

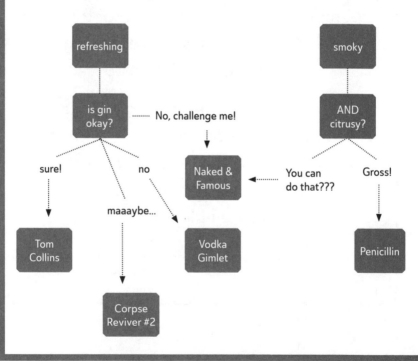

Once you realize that perhaps you like your Rob Roy with more vermouth, or your Daiquiri with more citrus than simple syrup, when you order one next time, you can politely tell the bartender that's what you like. Everybody wins!

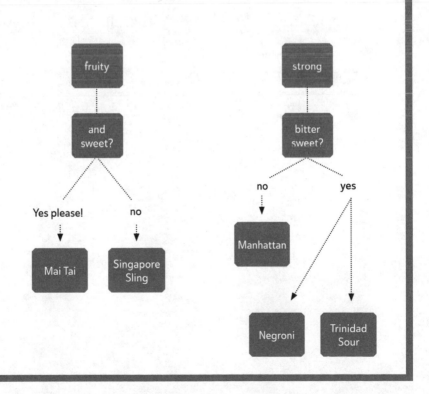

3

HOW TO MIX

Now you know a little bit about how and why we do things the way we do at our bar. No one really needs a professional bar at home, but we're here to help you learn how to stock and equip the home bar that's right for you. Whether you are slinging Daiquiris for your friends or stirring a Manhattan to enjoy on the couch with your cat—we've got you covered!

HOME BAR BASICS

A few years ago, Thea visited her nana's house for Christmas. Like a lady, she arrived with nothing but a bottle of bourbon. Her nana was downsizing and trying to clean out her fridge, so she told Thea to make whatever she wanted with whatever she could find. Thea accepted Nana's challenge.

She found, among other things, a bottle of crème de menthe, heavy cream, and a few eggs. Along with the bourbon brought from home, Thea mixed the heavy cream, an entire egg, and a touch of the crème de menthe (warning: it's a potent taste!) to make minty bourbon flips for her family. To be fair, they were all hesitant as they watched her throw an entire egg in the shaker, but they were happy with the result.

What's the moral of this story? Don't be afraid to experiment with what you've got! Nana's liquor cabinet was limited, but she had a few essentials: eggs and cream. You don't need a citrus or fancy mixers to make a delicious drink.

Sidebar: Lauren once tried to mix tequila with a melted freeze-pop on a beach trip. It was less successful.

BARTENDER SAYS

"My biggest tip for a home bar is to not think about what bottles or liquors you should buy, but what it is you like to drink. If you start with a cocktail that you like, get those ingredients so you can make that cocktail. Then do that for another cocktail and see where they overlap. Don't start with 'what bottles do I buy,' start with what you want to drink."

—Max Toste, Co-Owner of Deep Ellum, Cambridge, MA; Lone Star, Allston, MA; and Lone Star, Cambridge, MA

STOCK YOUR BAR

You too can be like Thea and Lauren. Here are some tools to keep on hand for when it's your moment to impress your friends and family:

- **Boston Shaker:** Those tins you see us mixing drinks in. Glass is popular to stir in, too, but it's more expensive (albeit prettier). You choose!

- **Bar Spoon:** Those long spoons you see us stirring with. Lauren stirs with her spoon in the drink; Thea stirs with the spoon upside down, like a damn animal. Deal with it. It's about preference and you should do whatever makes more sense to you.

- **Strainer:** Once you shake or stir the cocktail, if you don't want to use dirty ice, you need to strain without your fingers (don't be gross), so invest in one or all of the following types of strainers.

  - *Hawthorne Strainer:* The strainer with the coils. It essentially looks like it has a slinky on it. This is a pretty universal strainer, so you can't really go wrong with it.

  - *Julep Strainer:* The strainer that looks like a big spoon with a small handle and big holes in it. It's more commonly used for stirred cocktails, as there won't be huge ice chunks to strain out of a stirred cocktail. (If there is, you've made a mistake.) ▶

· *Tea Strainer:* A cone-shaped mesh strainer very often used to double-strain egg white drinks or shaken drinks as well. Some people want to get the ice chunks out of a shaken drink and will use the Hawthorne strainer as well as the tea strainer. That's about preference. This is a good tool to get mint bits out of a drink too!

▶ **Jigger:** Measuring device for fluid ounces. Again, choose the style you want—they come in all shapes and sizes and even with copper or gold plating!

▶ **Muddler:** A muddler is a wooden (but sometimes metal) tool you'll see behind the bar nowadays. It looks kind of like a tiny baseball bat with one end (meant for the muddling) that is flatter than the other. Of course, this changes based on the brand. It is used to help you crush ingredients (like mint leaves) to release the flavors. In this way, it gives you the opportunity to amp up the freshness of your drink.

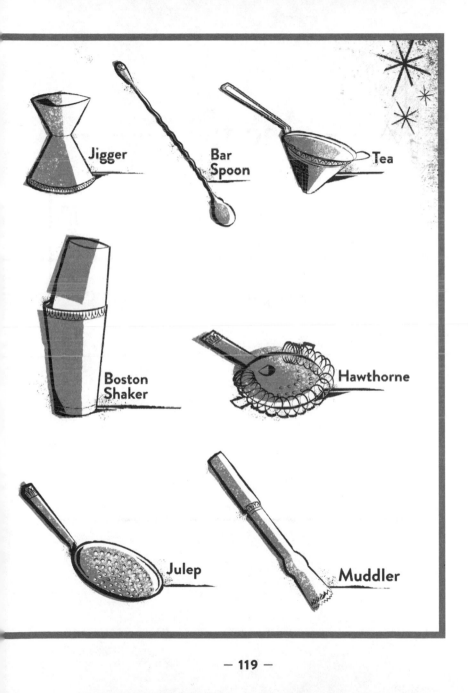

Jigger

Bar Spoon

Tea

Boston Shaker

Hawthorne

Julep

Muddler

PRO TIP

If your cocktail has juice in it, you shake it. That's the rule. Don't think twice about it. If it's straight spirit, stir. That's the rule. Don't think twice about it. Got it? Good. Now we're going to tell you that every rule has exceptions and this one does too. Sometimes the creator just wants the straight spirit cocktail to be shaken. Crazier things have happened! They will say so explicitly in their recipe.

THE GOOD STUFF

Just like *Ocean's Eleven* or any other stupid heist movie, when it comes to drink-making, you have key characters doing things that are apparently important. We've got the explosives expert, the tech person, the driver, and the dude who gets everyone together and somehow gets all the credit. Your home bar components are just like a bad movie.

Simple Syrup: Don't you dare buy this! You can make it at home in a few easy steps. It's equal parts hot water and sugar, stirred until the sugar dissolves. So, 1 cup sugar, 1 cup hot water, stir and stir. You can even add more sugar for a richer syrup, and in the winter, a brown sugar simple is nice to have around! This is a common ingredient in cocktails, especially Gimlets. It's a good idea to keep some in the fridge at all times. You can impress your friends by making some Gimlets on the fly (because of course you have those limes too). Just like sugar, simple doesn't expire. In fact, we use it in our coffee instead of sugar packets.

Sweet and/or Dry Vermouth: Thea's nana raised her to always be able to make her guests a Martini or Manhattan. Sweet vermouth goes in a Manhattan, dry vermouth in a Martini. But if you have both you can also make a Perfect Manhattan or a Perfect Martini, which uses a half ounce of each vermouth and will really impress your friends. ▶

Angostura Bitters: Get it, have it, love it. (Also great in soda water to cure a hangover.) Now made in Trinidad, Angostura bitters was created by a German doctor who moved to Venezuela in 1824 to be surgeon general of the army. Once there, he capitalized on the plethora of natural resources the country offered. Angostura bitters was named for the maritime trading town it was sold in. Translating to "the narrows," Angostura is known for its clove and cinnamon notes, secret recipe, and oversized label. The label was supposedly a silly misprint in the early days of printing, but became a signature that is still used in packaging today.

Peychaud's Bitters: This is lighter than Angostura, with more cherry and fewer warm notes. Peychaud's has deep roots in American cocktail history. It was created by a pharmacist in New Orleans, Antoine Peychaud, a Creole immigrant who used family recipes with his own well-versed knowledge of herbs to create what we now know as Peychaud's bitters. In 1838 he began selling his bitters in the French Quarter. Peychaud's is famous for its role in the classic cocktail the Sazerac, which is also credited as being America's first cocktail.

Campari: An amaro with strong orange notes. Campari is good to have in your bar because you can make anything from a low-alcohol, stomach-calming highball (Campari and soda), or classics like a Negroni for your gin-drinking guests and a Boulevardier for your whiskey-drinking guests.

Averna, Fernet, and/or Montenegro: Lauren's mom used to hand out cordials or digestifs after a dinner party. We still do the same, but prefer Averna or Montenegro over Drambuie or Sambuca. Not only are they great to mix with (like a Black Manhattan), but they are also nice to shoot or sip after a big meal. Host a big dinner, hand out one of these after, and blow some minds.

Basic Booze: Gin, bourbon, rye, tequila, and/or mezcal. You choose! Or have one of each—no judgment.

Citrus: Lime and/or lemon to juice, or pre-juiced juice (say that three times fast!), whatever you want. There's not much that can top a Daiquiri with fresh lime juice, and if you have lemon juice, gin, and soda water, you have a Tom Collins. Voilà!

Beer and Wine: You'll also want to stock some kind of craft beer you're into. Why not? Sometimes a person just wants to come home to a nice saison. Is that so much to ask? In the same vein, keep a bottle of wine on hand. It doesn't have to be expensive—it just has to be something you like. You're an adult, dammit, act like one!

PRO TIP

When you're trying to decide what garnish to use for a drink, whether it's a classic or your own recipe, just take a minute to think about the ingredients. For example: when Thea first started bartending, she kept mixing up her Sazerac and Negroni garnishes. She would always second-guess herself and look in her trusty recipe notebook to confirm before she would garnish either drink. Then one day it dawned on her: there is Campari in a Negroni. Campari is an amaro with orange notes. After that, it always made sense to her that the Negroni would have an orange peel. Why would you introduce lemon to a cocktail with no lemon notes in it? So when you're making something at home and you have to decide what to garnish it with, think about what matches the ingredients and what will enhance the flavors you've already put in the drink.

Sidebar: Also invest in Luxardo Maraschino Cherries. They're expensive, but damn they are delicious.

BAR BANTER

Egg whites are hot right now. But what do they really add to the drink other than a warning that consuming raw or undercooked food could result in foodborne illness? Some adjectives you're going to hear when egg white is involved: chewiness, texture, more body. It really just gives more rich body and creaminess to the cocktail. For example: Lauren's mom was the queen of whiskey sours.

Her secret? Egg white.

MECHANICS

Let's talk about the birds and the bees of bartending: shaking and stirring.

You are building a cocktail—let's say it's a Daiquiri. The rum, simple syrup, and lime go in the little guy shaker (the smaller half of your shaker). Then you take a scoop of ice with the big-boy shaker (the bigger half of your shaker), throw the ice into the little shaker, and lock the big shaker into the little shaker. Remember that you don't want them to be directly up and down. The two sides won't seal effectively that way. Make them crooked: the rim of the big half should be touching the side of the little half in one spot. Then smack the top with the heel of your hand until it locks. You are going to be throwing this bad boy around a little, after all. A poorly sealed shaker will split during the shaking process and that's a good way to get yourself sticky. We've both ended up with Tiki drinks in our hair. It happens to the best of us.

Now to unlock the shaker: hold the locked shakers in one hand so that your palm lines up with where the two halves meet. Take the heel of your other hand and hit the opposite side of the sealed shakers. It should unlock with one to three steady hits. Done!

ROOKIE MISTAKE

There's nothing worse than a wimpy shake—and no way to piss us off faster. Shake it hard, but not too long. Remember that there's ice in that shaker and ice does what, kids? It melts! Therefore, when you shake or stir for too long, you can dilute your drink and change the flavor. That being said, water is also an ingredient in your cocktail. It's a healthy balance (similar to how we don't go to the gym, but we think about it a lot—that counts, right?). Remember, you're shaking cold liquid and ice in metal so you're going to literally feel it getting colder. When you feel the temperature you want in your hands...stop. And that's it!

BARTENDER SAYS

"Don't waste booze by trying to do some fancy TGIFriday shit. You're putting liquid from one vestibule into another. It shouldn't be a ribbon dance routine. Use a jigger. Be precise."

—*Kim Bell, Bartender at The Publick House, Brookline, MA*

PRO TIP

Everybody has their own shake, and the truth is, it finds you. We know it sounds super lame to say that, but trust us, one day you will be shaking a cocktail and suddenly be in the kind of groove that feels better than when you were in the womb and your mom rocked back and forth and stared dreamily out the window, not considering the 18 years of sleepless nights ahead of her. Wait. What?

You don't have to worry so much about overstirring cocktails. Unlike shaking, the ice isn't chipping and melting quickly in the process. Still, you don't want to overstir. A good number of stirs to aim for is 40–50 turns.

INFUSIONS

It seems that your home bar is complete. You've chosen your spirit(s) and you have your simple syrup and some citrus. You may even have an amaro or fortified wine on hand. But you're like Eva Longoria in the early 2000s—you're hot and bored, dude! Don't cheat on us with a new hobby—just expand your horizons. Challenge yourself! The easiest way to do this is to mess with infusions and simple syrups.

Let's start with infusions! You can do so much with these, and we already mentioned how you can make vodka more interesting by throwing in some fruit, veggies, or, heck, even wood (that's right, we've done it!). So don't be shy!

There are some things you should keep in mind, though:

▶ **Don't break the bank with what you're infusing.** The important thing is the freshness of the produce you're using, not the price of the liquor. Definitely go well-quality with this.

▶ **Expose as much of the produce as possible.** What we mean is, don't just throw a strawberry in a jar of tequila; cut those strawberries up! Expose as much of their surface area to the tequila as possible.

- **Taste it daily and then strain when you like the way it tastes.** Yes, it's as simple as that. Keep in mind that season to season the produce can change. One year we had a lot of rain and it caused us to get these huge peaches, which were, unfortunately, not as flavorful as our usual smaller peaches. So we had to leave those peaches in our bourbon for several days longer than anticipated.

- **Consider the season when you're choosing what to infuse.** Strawberries and peaches are not going to be very fresh in winter. Even if you can buy them, that doesn't mean you should. You can also buy a DVD of *Hot Tub Time Machine*, but would you?

So now that you have the infusion, what do you do with it? Have fun! Get your head out of your ass and make some cocktails. If you've infused a tequila, consider your favorite tequila cocktail: would that pair well with what you've infused the tequila with?

BAR LINGO

Channel Knife: Similar to a vegetable peeler, but this has a smaller blade to make a twist versus a peel, which is a larger swath of fruit peel.

Twist: When you use a channel knife to peel a narrow spiral of fruit skin. A twist is actually twisted citrus peel, or, a long narrow rope of the peel only that is twisted into a corkscrew shape.

Peel or Swath: A much wider piece of citrus peel than a twist. A swath is just the zest (or colored part) of the citrus peel with ideally no pith or meat of the fruit at all.

Wedge: A slice of the fruit that is often shaped like a wedge or half-moon. This does involve the meat of the fruit. You can squeeze further citrus into your drink if you'd like. (Very commonly seen as a lime wedge on a Gin and Tonic, for example.)

PRO TIP

When making a twist, dig the channel knife into the skin of the fruit (not too deep, remember the pith is bitter) and turn the fruit, not the knife. You can make a twist as long as your arm when you do this correctly! (We've done it. It's awesome.)

PRO TIP

When you shake a cocktail, you incorporate a lot of air and small chips of ice into the drink. The shaking motion whips the cocktail (think of stirring a cup of cream versus whipping whipped cream) and breaks the ice down by knocking it into the sides of the shaker. When you stir a cocktail, the ice spins around in the center of your mixing glass as one continuous piece. It slowly melts into the drink to dilute it slightly, which softens and expands the flavors, and very little air is added. Stirring cocktails is what gives your Martinis and Manhattans that silky smooth mouthfeel, whereas shaking is what makes your Margarita so dang frothy. We'll get more into when to shake and when to stir later.

BAR BANTER

Because of its signature odorless and tasteless traits, vodka is easy to mix with and easily overpowered by citrus, liqueurs, fortified wines, and the like. As a result, many bartenders avoid making their own cocktails with vodka. It just doesn't offer much of a challenge. That being said, vodka has some really wonderful classic recipes and also offers up the opportunity for infusions. You can infuse fruit, vegetables, and spices with vodka or get creative with syrups to pair with it.

BARTENDER SAYS

"There's no shame in a well-crafted Cosmo. I'd take a Cosmo made with fresh lime and good triple sec any day over a Mojito made with not enough sugar and bruised mint. Of all the drinks that get shit, the Cosmo is the easiest to do well consistently!"

—*Robby MacNeil, Bartender at The Woodsman Tavern, Portland, OR*

COSMO

1½ oz. vodka
¾ oz. triple sec
½ oz. lime juice
Splash cranberry juice
Lime wheel for garnish

Add ingredients (except lime wheel) and ice to a cocktail shaker. Shake and strain into a chilled cocktail glass. Garnish with lime wheel.

VODKA GIMLET

2 oz. vodka
¾ oz. lime juice
½ oz. simple syrup

Add ingredients and ice to a cocktail shaker. Shake and strain into a chilled cocktail glass.

MOSCOW MULE

2 oz. vodka
½ oz. lime juice
3 oz. ginger beer
Lime wedge for garnish

Add vodka and lime juice to a copper mug or rocks glass. Top with ice and ginger beer. Garnish with lime wedge.

VESPER (A.K.A. THE JAMES BOND MARTINI)

2 oz. gin
1 oz. vodka
½ oz. Lillet Blanc
Lemon twist for garnish

Add all ingredients (except twist) and ice to a shaker and shake if you must, but we prefer to stir. Strain into a chilled cocktail glass and garnish with lemon twist.

SHAKE IT

A dry shake is when you put all your ingredients into the shaker and shake without ice. A wet shake is the opposite —it's when all your ingredients are shaken with ice.

So when do you use a dry shake and when do you use a wet shake? We're glad you asked!

You should use a dry shake when you are making a drink that is served over crushed ice. Do you remember what we said about dilution earlier—how shaking with ice dilutes the drink ever so slightly? Using a dry shake here prevents diluting a drink further (pouring it over crushed ice dilutes it as well).

Another good time to use a dry shake is when you are making a drink with egg white or a flip (a flip is a drink with an entire egg in it—yolk and all!). Dry shaking helps to emulsify the egg into the cocktail. Think about how you have to shake a bottle of vinaigrette dressing before you pour it. Before the shake, the ingredients don't want to hang out together. You need to shake them up really hard to mix and mingle. It's the same concept with eggs and egg whites. So make like Outkast and shake it like a Polaroid picture.

When you're still getting a feel for how long to dry shake, it's super helpful to add just one cube to the shaker. When you can't hear the cube shaking around anymore, it's time to add more ice.

PRO TIP

Don't buy expensive bottled cocktail mixers that are full of chemicals and sugar. You know the ones we're talking about. They come in plastic bottles and are sometimes created by chain restaurants. Yeah, *those*. Instead, take a stroll over to the frozen food aisle of your favorite grocery store. It's just as easy to throw some frozen fruit or a purée (maybe a can of coconut milk?) into a blender. Your cocktail will taste so much fresher than it would if you had used the bottled chemicals.

DAIQUIRI

2 oz. rum (usually white but definitely delicious with aged or agricole!)

¾ oz. lime juice

¾ oz. simple syrup

Add all ingredients and ice to a cocktail shaker. Shake and strain into a chilled coupe glass.

MAI TAI

1½ oz. white rum

1 oz. dark (aged) rum

¾ oz. triple sec

½ lime

¼ oz. orgeat (this is a French almond-based syrup—allergy alert—the good ones are made with real almonds!)

Dash Angostura bitters

Add all ingredients (except bitters) and ice to a shaker, shake, and strain over crushed ice in the most ridiculous glass you can find. Garnish with reckless abandon (pineapple chunk, cherry, orange wheel, etc.). Top with Angostura bitters.

AIRMAIL

1½ oz. aged rum (we like Barbancourt)
¾ oz. lime juice
¾ oz. honey syrup (equal parts honey and hot water)
1 oz. sparkling wine
Dash Angostura bitters
1 mint leaf for garnish

_____

Add rum, lime juice, honey syrup, and ice to a cocktail shaker. Shake and strain into a coupe glass. Top with sparkling wine and Angostura bitters. Garnish with mint leaf.

DARK & STORMY

4 oz. ginger beer
2 oz. dark rum (Gosling's is a great choice)
Lime wedge for garnish

_____

Add ice to a Collins or high-ball glass. Pour ginger beer into that bad boy. Add rum on top. Garnish with a lime wedge.

Dark & Stormy

MOJITO

About 6–10 mint leaves
4 lime wedges
1 sugar cube
Dash simple syrup (up to ½ oz. for taste) for a sweeter Mojito
2 oz. white rum
Splash soda water

Add mint, 3 lime wedges, sugar cube, and simple syrup to your shaker. Muddle ingredients, but not too much. Add rum and ice. Shake and dump entire contents, along with dirty rocks, into a Collins glass. Top with soda water. Garnish with the remaining lime wedge.

HEMINGWAY DAIQUIRI

1½ oz. white rum
¾ oz. lime juice
¼ oz. grapefruit juice
¼ oz. Maraschino liqueur
1 lime wedge for garnish

Add all ingredients (except lime wedge) and ice to a cocktail shaker and shake. Strain into a chilled coupe glass. Garnish with a lime wedge.

PRO TIP

A Dark & Stormy is beautiful in its simplicity. When you are making this cocktail, it's a great time to pay extra attention to the mixer you're using. The ginger beer you choose is extremely important here. Choose carefully and based on your own taste. Some ginger beers can be super spicy, and if you like that, embrace it. We really like AJ Stephans ginger beer, but Fever-Tree is also super popular. We just like more spice in our ginger beer (call us old-fashioned!).

1919

In case you were wondering, Punt e Mes is a delicious Italian vermouth, and Bénédictine is a French herbal liqueur. Both are amazing on their own as well as in cocktails.

¾ oz. Old Monk Rum
¾ oz. Rittenhouse rye
1 oz. Punt e Mes
½ oz. Bénédictine
Dash mole bitters

Add all ingredients and ice to a cocktail shaker or mixing glass. Stir and strain into a chilled cocktail glass.

CAIPIRINHA (THE NATIONAL DRINK OF BRAZIL)

½ lime (cut into wedges)
2 sugar cubes
2 oz. cachaça

Muddle the lime wedges with sugar cubes in a shaker. Add cachaça and ice. Shake it and then dump it all (dirty rocks, spent wedges) into a rocks glass.

BARTENDER SAYS

"One of my favorite things about being a bartender is that moment when someone is drinking something you've prepared for them, and they tell you how much they hate a particular spirit. Let's say…gin, for instance. They had a 'bad experience' with it in college. We've all been there. Not college, necessarily, but 'bad experiences,' they are universal. So you tell them that they are, indeed, *drinking gin*. It's fun to help people change perceptions, broaden their minds a bit, and see that in the right hands, prepared a certain way, a lively Eastside is a much different experience than that trash can gin punch they powered down at a toga party. So now they like gin. And the world is right."

—*Ryan Gannon, Bar Manager at Cure, New Orleans, LA*

TOM COLLINS/OLD TOM COLLINS

2 oz. gin or Old Tom Gin

½ oz. lemon juice (add ½ oz. orange juice if making Old Tom Collins)

½ oz. simple syrup

Splash soda water

Lemon wheel or cherry for garnish

_____

Add all ingredients (except soda water and garnish) to a cocktail shaker with ice and shake. Empty contents, dirty rocks and all, into Collins glass. Top with soda water. Garnish with lemon or cherry flag.

BEE'S KNEES

2 oz. gin

½ oz. lemon juice

½ oz. honey syrup

_____

Add ingredients to a cocktail shaker with ice and shake. Strain into a chilled coupe glass.

AVIATION

1½ oz. gin
½ oz. lemon juice
½ oz. Maraschino liqueur
½ oz. crème de violette
Maraschino cherry for garnish

Add all ingredients (except Maraschino cherry) to a cocktail shaker with ice and shake. Strain over a chilled cocktail glass. Add Maraschino cherry for garnish (just let it sink to the bottom).

Note: With a couple of modifications, this drink becomes something entirely different! Switch out that Maraschino liqueur for simple syrup and throw in an egg white, and you have an Eagle's Dream.

Go ahead and 86 that Maraschino cherry too. We like to garnish our egg white drinks with a couple of drops of Peychaud's bitters on top. Drag a toothpick or straw through the drops on top of the drink to make designs. It's not as hard as it looks and the bright pink of Peychaud's looks particularly nice on top of an Eagle's Dream!

LAST WORD

¾ oz. gin
¾ oz. Green Chartreuse
¾ oz. lime juice
¾ oz. Maraschino liqueur

_____

Add all ingredients to a cocktail shaker with ice and shake. Strain into a chilled cocktail glass.

RAMOS GIN FIZZ
(a.k.a. Most Pain in the Ass Drink)

This is a drink with a lot of history. It also has a lot of contemporary relevance in the restaurant industry. Since it's such a huge pain to make, often bartenders will order it from their friends just to be a pain. Isn't that cute? It is until it happens to you!

The Ramos Gin Fizz was invented in the late 1800s by Henry C. Ramos in a little town called New Orleans. It was called a New Orleans Fizz at first, and legend has it, the original recipe called for 15 minutes of shaking (we told you it was a pain!). In fact, some accounts note that in order to satisfy the demand for this drink, there were more than a dozen bartenders at a time making nothing but Ramos Gin Fizzes. Teams of bartenders had to shake the drink relay-style in order to achieve frothy perfection. So are you ready for the actual recipe now? More accurately, are your arms ready?

RAMOS GIN FIZZ

2 oz. gin
¾ oz. combined lemon and lime juice
¾ oz. simple syrup
1 oz. heavy cream
1 egg white
Dash orange blossom water
Splash soda water
Orange twist for garnish

Add all ingredients (except soda water and orange twist) to a cocktail shaker and shake. Dry shake for as long as you can last! We dare you! Then add ice and shake some more. Strain contents into Collins glass and top with soda water. The head of your drink should be super frothy and rise above the rim of the glass, like a soufflé. In fact, it should almost look like whipped cream.

Garnish with orange twist. Tell someone how sore your arms are.

CORPSE REVIVER #2

To start, pour a small amount (less than ¼ oz.) of absinthe or pastis into your chilled coupe and swirl glass around to coat. Dump out the excess. This is called a rinse and you can also do it with other spirits!

1 oz. gin
1 oz. Lillet Blanc or Cocchi Americano
1 oz. lemon juice
1 oz. orange liqueur (Combier or Cointreau will be best but triple sec if you must)

_____

Add ingredients to a cocktail shaker with ice and shake. Strain into chilled coupe glass with absinthe rinse.

NEGRONI

1 oz. gin
1 oz. Campari
1 oz. sweet vermouth
Orange swath for garnish

_____

Add ingredients and ice to a cocktail shaker or mixing glass. Stir and strain over chilled rocks glass. Express orange peel over finished cocktail.

AN ODE TO AGAVE

Lauren loves tequila. Lauren loves mezcal. Lauren loves a Tequila Gimlet (tequila, lime juice, simple syrup). Basically, if tequila or mezcal is involved, Lauren will try it, even if the other ingredients include cyanide. Thea's favorite way to enjoy tequila is to sip a nice reposado or shoot a silver. Lauren has also been known to shoot a tequila once or twice.

Thea is going to brag about Lauren's mad tequila and mezcal mixing skills. Lauren's mezcal and tequila drinks are consistently "bomb" as we said back in the day, kids. One of the best is her "Another Sun God" made with house-infused mezcal.

- ▶ **Step 1:** Get yourself some fresh marjoram, thyme, and French tarragon. Also get yourself a bottle of mezcal. (Bottom-shelf, remember—we're infusing, not pouring shots for the Queen!)

- ▶ **Step 2:** Put about a handful of each herb into a large jar. Top that jar off with your entire bottle of mezcal.

- ▶ **Step 3:** Walk away for 3–5 days, depending on how many herbs are in the jar. The more herbs the shorter the soak. Taste daily.

- ▶ **Step 4:** Strain. You now have a homemade infusion. We're so proud of you!

ANOTHER SUN GOD

¾ oz. herb-infused mezcal
¾ oz. reposado tequila (bottom-shelf tequila is fine)
¾ oz. lime juice
½ oz. Pierre Ferrand Dry Curaçao
½ oz. simple syrup
Pinch coarse salt

Add all ingredients (except salt) to a cocktail shaker with ice. Shake it! Serve over dirty rocks in a Double Old Fashioned glass. Top with coarse salt. Write Lauren a thank-you letter.

PALOMA

1½ oz. tequila (we prefer silver, but reposado works great too)
1½ oz. fresh-squeezed pink grapefruit juice
½ oz. fresh-squeezed lime juice
½ oz. simple syrup
Pinch salt
Splash soda water

Add ingredients (except soda water) to a cocktail shaker with ice and shake vigorously. Strain over fresh ice in a Collins or highball glass. Top with soda water.

MARGARITA

*If you like a salt rim on your Margarita, take a wedge
of lime and run it around the outside rim of your glass.
Dip the lip of the glass into a shallow dish of coarse
salt and gently shake off any extra. We then like to run
the lime wedge around the interior rim while holding
the glass upside down so that the salt is on the outside of the glass only. This will keep your cocktail from
tasting too salty.*

2 oz. tequila (or try it with mezcal!)
1 oz. fresh-squeezed lime juice
1 oz. triple sec

Add ingredients to a cocktail shaker with ice. Shake
vigorously and serve on the rocks or in a chilled
cocktail glass.

ROSITA

1½ oz. tequila (again, either silver or reposado would be lovely here)

½ oz. Campari

½ oz. dry vermouth (we like Dolin Dry)

½ oz. sweet vermouth (we like Dolin Rouge, but if you like your cocktails a touch sweeter go for Carpano Antica)

Dash Angostura bitters

Lemon twist for garnish

Add all ingredients (except twist) and ice to a cocktail shaker or mixing glass. Stir and serve on the rocks with a lemon twist.

CONQUISTADOR

1 oz. reposado tequila

1 oz. aged rum (we like El Dorado 8-Year or Plantation Original Dark)

¾ oz. fresh-squeezed lemon/lime juice (combined)

¾ oz. simple syrup

2 dashes orange bitters

1 egg white

Add ingredients to a cocktail shaker with ice and shake vigorously for several seconds. (This will incorporate the egg white into your drink.) Fill shaker with ice and shake again. Strain into a chilled cocktail glass.

PRO TIP

Yes, Chartreuse is expensive. If you don't want to invest in a bottle for your home bar, but do want a similar flavor profile, look for Dolin Génépy des Alpes. It's also French, but it isn't made by monks. It's very similar in taste, but lighter and a lot cheaper.

NAKED & FAMOUS

¾ oz. mezcal
¾ oz. Aperol
¾ oz. lime
¾ oz. Yellow Chartreuse

Add ingredients to a cocktail shaker with ice. Shake and serve on the rocks in a rocks glass.

DIVISION BELL

1 oz. mezcal
¾ oz. Aperol
¾ oz. lime juice
½ oz. Maraschino liquer
Grapefruit twist for garnish

Add all ingredients (except twist) to cocktail shaker with ice and shake. Strain into a cocktail glass and garnish with grapefruit twist.

OAXACAN OLD FASHIONED

¼ oz. agave
2 dashes mole bitters
Splash soda water
1½ oz. reposado tequila
¾ oz. mezcal
Orange peel

Add ingredients (except orange peel) to a cocktail shaker or mixing glass. Add ice and stir until sugar is dissolved. Pour into rocks glass. Garnish with a flamed orange peel.*

*Wait, what? Yep, that's right—a flamed orange peel! You can do this with any citrus peel. Simply peel the zest off an orange with a Y-shaped vegetable peeler (try to avoid the pith—the bitter white part between the peel and fruit) and hold the peel over the cocktail with the outside facing the drink. Light a match and very gently squeeze the peel toward the flame (be sure not to squeeze the peel too hard or you will break it in half). The oil from the peel will ignite over the cocktail in a small burst and impart a slightly smoky, citrusy zest flavor.

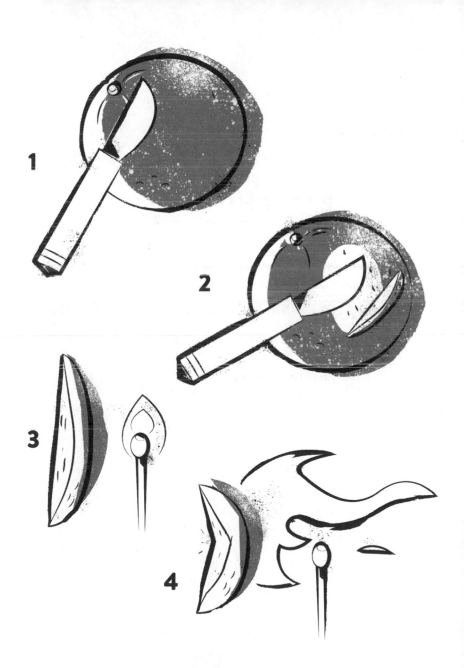

BARTENDER SAYS

"Like love, mezcal is complex from the production to the flavor, and like a kiss, it goes from the lips straight to your heart."

—Brian Beattie, Director of Operations at Deep Ellum, Allston, MA; Lone Star, Allston, MA; and Lone Star, Cambridge, MA

PRO TIP

Here's a fun game: try to replace the base spirit in your favorite cocktail with mezcal! For example: a Mezcal Gimlet, Mezcal Margarita, Mezcal Negroni, Mezcal Mule, all bomb.

BARTENDER SAYS

"Sweet vermouth is usually overlooked in the importance of a cocktail. Different ones can completely change the game for your Negroni, Manhattan, Boulevardier, etc. Take some time to experiment with different brands to see which ones will make the best version of the cocktail you want!"

—Mika Gagné, Bartender at Saraghina, Brooklyn, NY

OUR FAVORITE MANHATTAN

2½ oz. rye whiskey
¾ oz. sweet vermouth
3 dashes Angostura bitters
Maraschino cherry for garnish

———————

Add ingredients (except cherry) and ice to a
cocktail shaker or mixing glass. Stir and strain
into a chilled cocktail glass. Garnish with cherry.

BOULEVARDIER

1 oz. bourbon
1 oz. sweet vermouth
1 oz. Campari
Orange swath for garnish

———————

Add ingredients (except swath) and ice to a cocktail
shaker or mixing glass. Stir and strain into a chilled
cocktail glass. Garnish with orange swath.

BLACK MANHATTAN

2½ oz. bourbon
¾ oz. Averna

Add all ingredients and ice to cocktail shaker or mixing glass. Stir and strain into chilled cocktail glass.

Manhattan

SAZERAC

1 sugar cube
4–6 dashes Peychaud's (some purists will say less, more like 2)
Splash soda water
2 oz. rye (Sazerac rye in this is divine)
1 oz. absinthe (of Herbsaint if you're a New Orleans purist)
Lemon swath

Add sugar cube to your tin or mixing glass (per personal preference) and add Peychaud's. Muddle the Peychaud's and cube until the cube is granulated. Add the slightest dash of soda water to help dissolve the sugar. Add rye and ice and stir until sugar is dissolved. Rinse a chilled Old Fashioned glass with absinthe and strain cocktail into Old Fashioned glass. Make a lemon swath. Express it over the cocktail (squeeze until a mist of juice is released) and rub the peel on the rim of the glass. Drop swath into cocktail.

OLD FASHIONED

The first thing you should be asked (or asking, if you are making it) when ordering an Old Fashioned is if you have a whiskey preference. Very often people like bourbon with their Old Fashioned, but it really depends on your taste. The second thing you should be asked (or asking) is whether you want fruit. This means "do you want the bartender to muddle a cherry and orange wedge along with your sugar cube while making the drink?" Say yes if you want it, but the original recipe does not call for it.

1 sugar cube
2 dashes Angostura bitters
Splash soda water
2 oz. whiskey of choice
Orange swath for garnish

Place sugar cube in an Old Fashioned glass and drown it with Angostura bitters. Muddle the sugar cube and bitters until the sugar cube is granulated. Add a small splash of soda water to the sugar and bitters to help dissolve the sugar. Add whiskey and ice and stir until sugar is dissolved. Garnish with orange swath.

FRENCH 75

We have two different schools of thought on a French 75. Firstly, let us doubly confuse you by telling you that the original French 75 was made with cognac, not gin. But not many people drink it that way anymore. Now that that's out of the way, we can tell you that some people like their French 75 on the rocks in a Collins glass and some people prefer it in a Champagne flute. The former will obviously dilute with the ice and also have a teensy bit more bubbles, but your preference is your preference. We're not here to judge (for that at least...).

1½ oz. gin
½ oz. lemon juice
½ oz. simple syrup
1 oz. Prosecco or Cava (no need to waste good Champagne on a mixed drink)
Lemon twist for garnish

Add all ingredients (except twist and Prosecco or Cava) and ice to a cocktail shaker and shake. Strain into Champagne flute and top with bubbles (Cava or Prosecco). Garnish with lemon twist.

TRINIDAD SOUR

1½ oz. Angostura bitters
½ oz. Rittenhouse rye
1 oz. orgeat almond syrup
¾ oz. lemon juice

—————

Add ingredients to a cocktail shaker with ice and shake. Strain into a chilled coupe.

DE LA LOUISIANE (A.K.A. LA LOUISIANE)

2 oz. rye
¾ oz. Bénédictine
¾ oz. sweet vermouth
3 dashes absinthe
3 dashes Peychaud's
Maraschino cherry for garnish

—————

Add ingredients (except cherry) and ice to a cocktail shaker or mixing glass. Stir and strain into a chilled cocktail glass. Garnish with Maraschino cherry.

PAPER PLANE

¾ oz. bourbon
¾ oz. Aperol
¾ oz. Amaro Nonino
¾ oz. lemon juice
Lemon twist for garnish

Add all ingredients (except twist) to a cocktail shaker with ice and shake. Strain into a chilled coupe and add lemon twist garnish.

RED HOOK

2 oz. rye
½ oz. Punt e Mes
½ oz. Maraschino liqueur

Add all ingredients and ice to a cocktail shaker or mixing glass and stir. Strain into a chilled cocktail glass.

OLD PAL

1 oz. rye
1 oz. dry vermouth
1 oz. Campari
Orange swath for garnish

Add all ingredients (except swath) and ice to a cocktail shaker or mixing glass and stir. Strain into a chilled cocktail glass and garnish with orange swath.

TORONTO

2 oz. rye whiskey
½ oz. Fernet-Branca
½ oz. simple syrup

Add ingredients and ice to a cocktail shaker or mixing glass. Stir and strain into a chilled cocktail glass.

WHISKEY SMASH

The Whiskey Smash has been around for pretty much as long as people have been slinging drinks. The exact measurements are different wherever you go, and even the juice involved changes. Definitely mess with proportions and juices to see what you like.

6 mint leaves
4 lemon wedges
2 oz. bourbon
½ oz. simple syrup
Mint sprig for garnish

Put mint leaves and lemon wedges in shaker. Muddle, but do not muddle too long. The mint will become bitter if over-muddled. Add remaining ingredients and ice. Shake and double-strain (use Hawthorne strainer over tea strainer to separate all the tiny mint-bits) into a rocks glass. Add crushed ice. Garnish with mint sprig.

VIEUX CARRÉ

1 oz. rye
1 oz. cognac
1 oz. sweet vermouth
Dash (⅛ oz.) Bénédictine
Dash Angostura bitters
Dash Peychaud's bitters
Orange swath for garnish

Add ingredients (except swath) and ice to a cocktail shaker or mixing glass. Stir and strain into a chilled cocktail glass. Garnish with orange swath.

BLOOD AND SAND

¾ oz. Scotch
¾ oz. Punt e Mes
¾ oz. orange juice
¾ cherry Heering liqueur

Add ingredients to a cocktail shaker with ice. Shake and strain into a chilled cocktail glass.

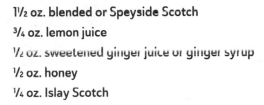

PENICILLIN

1½ oz. blended or Speyside Scotch
¾ oz. lemon juice
½ oz. sweetened ginger juice or ginger syrup
½ oz. honey
¼ oz. Islay Scotch

_____

Add ingredients (except Islay Scotch) and ice to a cocktail shaker and shake. Serve on the rocks with float (about ¼ oz.) of Islay Scotch on top.

ROB ROY

2½ oz. Scotch
1 oz. sweet vermouth
2 dashes Angostura bitters
Maraschino cherry for garnish

_____

Add ingredients (except cherry) and ice to a cocktail shaker or mixing glass and stir. Strain into a cocktail glass. Garnish with Maraschino cherry. *Sound familiar? Good! It's just a Manhattan with Scotch. You've learned something!*

THE BLACK LODGE

Before you can assemble this drink, you'll need to do a little work.

▸ **This recipe yields how much bourbon you use—this could be 1 liter or it could be 7 liters. It just depends on how much you want!**

1. Purchase a bag of applewood chips from the grill section of the hardware store (or online—come on). You need enough to fill a glass jar halfway.

2. Purchase a glass jar.

3. Char the woodchips on your grill or in your oven on the broiler setting. (Make sure you open all the windows first, and be ready to set the fire alarm off or at least have everything in your house smell like campfire for a week—Lauren has a very understanding boyfriend.)

4. While the woodchips are still smoking, carefully pour them into the jar.

5. Once any flames have gone out, but while the chips are still smoking, carefully pour bourbon on top (no need to break the bank here, Four Roses or Jim Beam will do just fine). Don't add the bourbon while the chips are still on fire unless you're making a Molotov cocktail.

6. Infuse for 3–4 days. Taste it daily and give the jar a shake, and then strain and store in a clean jar or bottle.

To make the cocktail:

2 oz. Charred Applewood Bourbon (the one you just made!)
½ oz. brown sugar syrup (2 parts brown sugar dissolved in 1 part hot water)
1¼ oz. Guinness

In a mixing glass, add ice, bourbon, and brown sugar syrup and stir. Pour Guinness into a chilled rocks glass. Strain bourbon mixture on top of Guinness.

ROOKIE MISTAKE

White wine is not always made from white grapes. The biggest difference between white and red wines is that white wine grapes are pressed to remove their juice from their skins prior to fermentation. Chardonnay is made from white grapes, whereas Pinot Grigio is made from purple grapes. Have we blown your mind yet?

FOOLPROOF SANGRIA

1 pineapple, cut into chunks

6 oz. lemon juice

12 oz. orange juice

16 oz. triple sec

8 oz. brandy (we like Christian Brothers; get something inexpensive, but don't you dare use a fruit-flavored "brandy")

8 oz. simple syrup

2 bottles dry red wine (or a box; go for the cheap stuff, but don't use anything you wouldn't drink on its own)

Splash soda water

In a large pitcher, add pineapple and muddle. Add lemon juice, orange juice, triple sec, brandy, simple syrup, and red wine. Stir, stir, stir! Then add ice and stir some more. Serve over ice, topped with a splash of soda water.

LEFT BANK

1½ oz. gin
1 oz. St-Germain liqueur
1 oz. Sauvignon Blanc
Lime twist for garnish

———————————

Add ingredients (except twist) and ice to a cocktail shaker and shake. Strain into a chilled cocktail glass. Garnish with lime twist.

NY SOUR

2 oz. bourbon
¾ oz. lemon juice
¾ oz. simple syrup
½ oz. Malbec

———————————

Add all ingredients (except Malbec) and ice to a cocktail shaker and shake. Strain over fresh ice in a rocks glass. Pour Malbec over the back of a spoon to float on top of the cocktail.

ROOKIE MISTAKE

So you made a drink too strong. Do *not* panic! Now what? Waste it? What are you, some kind of billionaire? Don't throw that away! Take a step back and give your drink a taste. Could you add more citrus to brighten it? Lime juice is always good for that. What could help balance out the booze? How about a dash of soda water? Could you simply put it on the rocks, add some simple syrup, fortified wine, or St-Germain? Have fun with it! Even if it doesn't taste good, it will be a learning experience.

THE HARD
TRUTH

Guys, there's something we need to tell you: we are not your parents. We do not have to love you no matter what, even if you're going to tip us. If you're rude or condescending, we pick up on it very quickly and your service will suffer for it. It's human nature.

Sometimes there are things a guest does that we will snicker about later. But some things will make us downright angry.

Remember that we want you to be happy and comfortable and we work every moment toward that. We consider you our guests and we want you to enjoy yourself, *but*, as a guest you must respect our rules. This is still our house.

ROOKIE MISTAKE

Don't buy expensive vodka simply because it's expensive. That's actually good advice regarding all spirits, and everything else in your life. (Look at us! Life coaches over here.) Vodka drinkers seem to be particularly guilty of this. Try tasting a few alongside each other (with no mixers, thank you) and see for yourself which you prefer.

BARTENDER SAYS

"Vodka: the more it costs
the more it tastes like water."

—*Erika Olson, Server at The Independent, Somerville, MA*

ROOKIE MISTAKE

Do not drink flavored vodka. Please don't make us repeat ourselves. It's just basic logic: if you have to be 21 to drink, don't drink something that tastes like candy. Did you know there's such a thing as Swedish Fish–flavored vodka?! Its very existence is an insult to you and your bartender. Remember that when someone is privileged enough to stand behind that bar, they should be able to make something delicious and fresh, not something chemically infused that can just be tossed into Red Bull or soda water.

TO SIP OR NOT TO SIP

Sipping on rum straight isn't really common in America, but there's no need to judge someone if that's what they want. We're in a safe judgment-free zone here. Most often, whiskeys are sipped. Everything from bourbon to Scotch is often sipped neat, but any spirit is fair game here. The best way to really appreciate a well-crafted product is to just sip it unadulterated.

And for the record, if you're debating over a kind of rum to have in a cocktail and the bartender offers up something you've never had, there's absolutely no reason why you can't get a tiny taste of it before it's put in something you're paying for.

PRO TIP

Just because you don't know or can't remember the proper term for a liquor, cocktail, or glass, doesn't mean you have to stay quiet. Feel free to try to explain to the bartender what you'd like. For example, if you can't remember that you like your Manhattan down, tell them you want it in a stemless glass with no ice. Simple as that!

Warning: Do not say you don't want your drink in a "girly glass." That's offensive. Don't be an idiot.

BARTENDER SAYS

"I find it really tacky when people refer to drinks as being girly, or make fun of a dude in their party for getting a drink in a coupe or Martini glass. Sometimes, all you want is a cold drink with a bunch of juice in it. Go for it. Nine times out of 10, when I sit down at a bar I'm ordering a Daiquiri first. Also, James Bond drank Martinis."

—*Stephen Konrads, Bartender at River Bar, Somerville, MA*

ROOKIE MISTAKE

Martinis are a stirred cocktail, made with either gin or vodka, traditionally gin. Martinis are not filled with chocolate, apple, or espresso, sweet child. Martinis do *not* equal cocktails. That's a weird thing that happened in the 1990s—like platform sandals and butterfly clips. We've been trying to get away from it ever since. Cut us a break!

Martini

MUDDLE YOUR WAY INTO OUR HEARTS

There's a common joke that Mojitos are a pain in the ass to make because of the muddling process. The truth is, they just plain aren't hard to make. In fact, they shouldn't be muddled too much because over-muddling makes the mint bitter. We digress... What is a pain? When you ask the bartender what she recommends, because you usually drink a Mojito, and she pours her heart out about classic cocktails—specifically her own personal variation she likes to make a regular who also loves Mojitos—and gives you a taste of different white rums, all resulting in you making a pinched-up face and saying, "I'll just have a rum and Coke." Come on! If you just want a basic highball, tell us that. We have other guests to get to, we have bottles to clean, we have kegs to change. Remember, judgment comes from how you act, not what you order. Unless it's a Long Island Iced Tea...or flavored vodka.

ROOKIE MISTAKE

Don't be fooled! Sloe gin is not a gin! It's actually a liqueur made from sloe berries, which are wild plums. This is going to be a lot darker in color, one might say "plum colored" even. It's also significantly sweeter than gin and doesn't taste like juniper. And why is that, class? Because it isn't a gin at all!

BAR BANTER

Sexism in bar culture goes back a long time. For example, gin was all the rage in the United Kingdom in the 1700s. It was dirt cheap and sold almost everywhere. People were drinking dangerous amounts of it, which caused politicians to intervene. They led a campaign saying that gin consumption had become deadly (probably true) and that it was making women infertile and causing them to ignore and abandon their existing children (probably less true). Despite the fact that men and women alike were drinking gin, the spirit was referred to as "Mother's Ruin." The demonization of female gin drinkers was just another drop in the Martini (see what we did there?) in a long line of sexism in bar culture.

ROOKIE MISTAKE

The only difference between a
Tom Collins and a Gin Fizz is the garnish
and the glass. A Tom Collins is served
in a Collins glass (duh) and a Gin Fizz is
served in a rocks glass with no garnish.
In case you were wondering, a Gin Fizz,
traditionally called a Silver Fizz, is also
served in a Collins glass, but has no ice
and the addition of an egg white. Do you
have a headache yet? No? Okay then,
say it ten times fast!

BAR BANTER

Julia Child was famously in love with vermouth. She was known to drink a sort of "reverse Martini," which was mostly vermouth with very little gin. Homegirl had good taste, what can we say! This habit was the inspiration for Thea's original cocktail, the Rose Tyler. The Rose Tyler was on the opening menu for River Bar, a craft cocktail–focused bar that we opened together in 2014. Thea was working on the cocktail and couldn't figure out what it was missing when Lauren walked by, took one sip, and said "St-Germain." Don't ever say we don't complete each other.

ROSE TYLER

1¼ oz. Cocchi Rosa
1 oz. Lillet Rose
½ oz. St-Germain liqueur
½ oz. gin

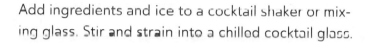

Add ingredients and ice to a cocktail shaker or mixing glass. Stir and strain into a chilled cocktail glass.

PRO TIP

Here's the honest truth. We have a secret. We're big proponents of simple cocktails made with fresh ingredients, but sometimes all you need in life is a giant frozen Strawberry Margarita. If it's bigger than your head and the color of a unicorn's birthday cake, it probably came out of a plastic bottle (or better yet, a bag) and was poured directly into a slush machine. It contains more calories than the aforementioned unicorn birthday cake, and will probably give you a massive headache the next day, but for that one glorious moment all will be right in the world. Pairs well with the greasiest tortilla chips you can get your hands on.

BAR BANTER

Despite the sexy name, the Margarita probably wasn't named after a woman. In the mid-late 1800s, a cocktail called the "Daisy" was popular. It consisted of spirit, citrus, and a liqueur used as a sweetener. A popular version combined gin, lemon, and orange liqueur. When tequila was subbed for gin, and lime for lemon juice, the name was changed to Margarita: the Spanish word for daisy.

ROOKIE MISTAKE

Do not mix bottled Margarita mix with good tequila. Just don't. Beside the fact that it's full of hangover-inducing sugar, the artificial flavors in the mix will overpower all of the subtleties of the tequila. A Margarita is one of the simplest cocktails in the world to make. It's three ingredients, people! Buy a bag of limes and an orange liqueur and impress your friends.

BARTENDER SAYS

Question: "What is one mistake
you see new bartenders make the most?"
Answer: "Not asking enough questions and
trying to wing something so they don't look
stupid. Trust me, you look way worse when
you serve someone a bastardized version
of what they actually wanted."

—*Kim Bell, Bartender at The Publick House, Brookline, MA*

ROOKIE MISTAKE

Don't assume tequila needs to be paired with citrus. Remember that it's wonderful in a stirred drink as well. If you like tequila, you should have a bottle of the style of your choice to sip on or mix with, a fresh lime or two, and of course sugar and water to make yourself some simple syrup on the fly. (Once again, don't you dare purchase simple syrup—we taught you better!)

BAR BANTER

Blanton's whiskey was one of only a handful of distilleries allowed to continue producing alcohol during Prohibition. Col. Blanton favored one warehouse on the premise in particular, Warehouse H, because he believed the bourbon it produced always tasted better. He was right—the combination of its proximity to the Kentucky River and metal walls allowed for optimal aging. Today, you can buy Single-Barrel Bourbon from Warehouse H (and it's amazing) but back in the day, Col. Blanton reserved the bourbon from that warehouse for VIPs like ambassadors (which might be how he got the government to allow him to produce alcohol during Prohibition).

ROOKIE MISTAKE

Flex your obscure whiskey-knowledge muscles appropriately. Yes, Bulleit is delicious. Yes, Prichard's is pretty much proof that there is a higher being, but dude, if you mix that with Coke, you lose all the respect knowing the brand gets you. We respect someone who orders a Jim Beam and Coke more than someone who orders a Prichard's and Coke. It's like you're spitting in our face when you corrupt a beautiful whiskey with soda!

BAR BANTER

Canadian whiskey became popular in America during Prohibition because it was illegal for most distillers (remember Blanton's was allowed to produce) to continue distilling during this time. Therefore, American bootleggers would make runs up to Canada to transport and sell whiskey to thirsty Americans. After Repeal Day, December 5, 1933, America made great strides in distilling and brewing its own craft products, pretty much ending the demand for Canadian whiskey in the United States.

PRO TIP

Whiskey has inspired and continues to inspire distillers all around the world. It is made in many different countries by many different amazing people. What we outline in this book are simply the big 5 styles that you will encounter in most American bars today, but you can find whiskey from Germany, Austria, and France, to name a few. What a time to be alive!

BREAKING DOWN GENDER NORMS, ONE DRINK AT A TIME

Whiskey tends to have a reputation as a "man's drink," but that's sexist and outdated. Most of the women we know are whiskey drinkers. In fact, we both agree that whiskey is our favorite spirit.

Let us tell you why: We love whiskey because of its history. It goes so far back that it can hardly be traced back to any one person or any place in particular. We love whiskey for its tasting notes: toffee, oak, smoke, chocolate, caramel, leather, peat. We love whiskey for its constant evolution. Age it longer, age it under water, age it on boats, make it with only one grain, make it with four different grains—taste the difference! So mostly we love whiskey because each whiskey is like a piece of art: it is crafted, it is hated, it is loved, rejected, revised, and given time and sweat and tears. And then it is given to us to enjoy. How beautiful is that?

Its flavor is complex and there are so many varieties to choose from! Just like with Girl Scout cookies, sometimes you want one kind, other times you want a different kind. Okay, 90% of the time we want Samoas, but we're not going to let that stop us from buying Thin Mints...oooo, or those little shortbread ones you dunk in your coffee...

ROOKIE MISTAKE

Jameson is not the only Irish whiskey you should drink. We promise there are many Irish whiskeys that will knock your socks off. Redbreast, Yellow Spot, and Green Spot are some of our favorite Irish whiskeys. Expand your horizons, people!

BAR BANTER

Templeton whiskey has been affectionately called "The Good Stuff" since it was created and sold illegally in 1920. It was Al Capone's whiskey of choice and legend has it, bottles of Templeton made it to Capone during his stint at Alcatraz. Templeton wasn't produced legally until 2001, 68 years after Repeal Day.

ROOKIE MISTAKE

It's a common misconception that whiskey can or should only be enjoyed when the weather is cold. Why? Sure, we prefer strong and stirred whiskey cocktails, but whiskey is also really fabulous in a shaken cocktail. It's a versatile spirit and deserves to be consumed all year round.

BAR BANTER

Don't for a second think that creating liquor is an easy process. For example, while creating Balvenie Caribbean Cask, a most delicious Scotch, the Malt Master first created his own blend of select Caribbean rums to fill the casks with before aging the Scotch in them. This meant he could get the desired flavor profile from the Balvenie Scotch he would eventually age within those same casks.

Holy dedication, Batman.

PRO TIP

"Sour mash" whiskey does not mean that the whiskey tastes sour in any way. Sour mash refers to a process where some of a previous batch of whiskey (before it's been distilled, when it's still essentially "beer") is added to a new batch to kick-start fermentation.

For those of you who are bakers, this process is similar to the use of a sourdough starter in breadmaking. Most bourbon is sour mash whiskey.

BARTENDER SAYS

"My go-to drink is always a Last Word, or one
of its magical variations. Naked and Famous is
an underappreciated Last Word variation,
I think. Mezcal and Aperol play beautifully
together, and make that drink one of my
favorite hot summer day drinks. Also
Becherovka over Fernet-Branca any
day of the week. Becky is life."

—*Tania Ross, Bartender at Bramling Cross, Seattle, WA*

BAR BANTER

It feels appropriate to note that there is a dangerous line to walk when looking at fruit beers. You can tell we love sours and all the weird, fruity notes in them. However, we caution you to order "fruit" beers carefully. You are entering the danger zone of loads of sugar and mystery ingredients. Take a minute to consider what you're ordering. Is it a fruit beer from a brewery that's so enormous it's actually several breweries? Do you think that's *real* fruit in there? Is it brewed in a German brewery that's been making beer for longer than the United States has existed? Do you think there's real fruit in *there*? Yes, there is. Use your brain.

ROOKIE MISTAKE

When it comes to beer, there is one thing we will never quite understand: pumpkin beer with a cinnamon sugar rim. Don't get us wrong: we like a good robust autumn-inspired beer. But come on! How many times do we have to stress this, people: *alcohol is for grownups*! And let's be clear here: a pumpkin beer with a cinnamon rim is *much* different than a Mexican lager and a lime. A Mexican lager like Sol, Corona, or Tecate can be enhanced with the brightness of a lime. Also, making a cinnamon sugar plate to dip your pint glasses in is messy, sticky, and a pain in the ass. Please don't make us!

THE SHANDY

Don't buy a bottled shandy. Shandies originated in Europe and are defined as beer mixed with lemonade, ginger beer, or both. Nowadays, Shandies are on menus all over the place and don't necessarily have lemonade or ginger in them. Heck, we've even seen beer involved in a stirred cocktail or two. (Lauren even created one of those! See the recipe for The Black Lodge in Part 3.) If you buy a premade Shandy, you are probably buying a lot of sugar and syrup. But you guys know better than that now, right? Here are some tips for making a Shandy at home:

Stuff You Need:

1. A light beer is good to start with and easy to mix with. It definitely doesn't need to be fancy. We'd recommend any macro lager like a Miller High Life.

2. You already have fresh citrus in your fridge (right?). Lemon works well with Shandies, as they originated with lemonade.

3. Simple syrup (you know better than to buy this).

4. Ginger or ginger-flavored something. It could be literal gingerroot or ginger beer, or it could be a ginger liqueur like Domaine de Canton. (Expensive but delicious!)
   If you have gingerroot, you should skin it, cut it up into really small pieces, and give it a muddle in your Shandy. If you have gingerroot and a couple of days to kill, you should do the same and let it sit in simple syrup for a few days. Taste daily, then strain when it's got the flavor you're looking for.

HOME SHANDY

▸ **Build this one in a pint glass.**

³/₄ oz. lemon juice

½ oz. simple syrup (use less if you're using ginger simple or ginger liqueur—those will add sweetness!)

½–1 oz. ginger flavoring of your choice (add more or less to taste)

4 oz. lager of your choice

In your cocktail shaker, add ice, lemon juice, simple syrup, and ginger flavoring. Shake! Add more ice and then top with your lager of choice.

MACRO BEERS

There's nothing wrong with macro beers, a.k.a. domestics. They definitely have a place on the scene and a place in our heart. There are plenty of instances where grabbing a cheap, crisp lager is appropriate—we do it too. But do not judge a bar for not carrying your brand of macro. There is no reason for a bar to carry every single macro in the world, just like they wouldn't carry every single French wine there ever was. So in other words, if you ask for a Miller Lite, and we say we don't carry it, but we do have Bud Light, don't you dare roll your eyes at us. Just drink your low-calorie beer and be on your way. For reference, our favorite macros are Budweiser and Miller High Life.

BAR BANTER

Orange wines are currently the new hotness. Contrary to what the name may lead you to believe, they're not made from oranges, nor are they always orange in color (though many of them are). They're made in the same way as rosé, but the pressed grape juice is left to macerate on white grape skins rather than red. Orange wines tend to be on the funky side, and a lot of them are pretty pricy, but they're interesting and a lot of fun. Definitely try one if you have the opportunity. Just don't expect it to taste like a white wine—they're tannic and taste more like reds without the color. What a fun way to mess with your friends!

─ ROOKIE MISTAKE ─

You may have heard that wine improves with age. Wrong. Some wines, such as some lighter reds and rosés, are often better when young. In fact, most wines are meant to be consumed within 5 years. Some big, tannic wines and Champagnes age beautifully. At any rate, live by the bartender's code: "You can't take it with you." (That's something only bartenders say, right?) It's nice to cellar something for a special occasion, but don't let hoarding wine get in the way of actually drinking the wine. The drinking is the fun part.

BARTENDER SAYS

"A good bartender can put anybody as equally at ease as they can in their place. That's the point of hospitality: to let people know they're at your place."

—*Max Toste, Co-Owner of Deep Ellum, Allston, MA; Lone Star, Allston, MA; and Lone Star, Cambridge, MA*

SPEAK UP!

Here's the thing: When we try to take your order and you say, "Um...what do you like to drink?" or "What's your favorite drink to make?" you *might* end up getting a funny look from our side of the bar. Our favorite drink to make is the one that will make you the happiest, and we probably have very different taste than you do. Instead, try giving us an idea of what you like and letting us make suggestions. Say something like, "I want something refreshing and citrusy, and I don't care for rum."

BARTENDER SAYS

"People, believe it or not, we *like* you. The bartender does not hate you. You pay our rent. You keep us company. You make us feel cool even though we're doing a job that does not require rock star qualifications, despite our ostensive belief that this is not the case."

—*Kim Bell, Bartender at The Publick House, Brookline, MA*

MESSAGE FROM THE AUTHORS

Well, you've read the book and gotten a small glimpse into the world of bartending and restaurants. We hope you've enjoyed the wild ride through wine, beer, and spirits.

This book would not have been possible without Ken Kelly, whose aspirations as a restaurant owner created the space in which we met. And whose ambition in the industry and faith in hard work and creativity continue to inspire us. For Jess Willis, who hired us, trained us, and promoted us. Thank you for believing in us, thank you for making us the right amount of pretentious, and thank you for being our friend. For Eileen, whose patience as an editor and—dare we say—friend is immeasurable. Thank you.

If you can't tell, we are lovers of alcohol. We love learning about it, drinking it, and getting drunk with it (and each other). But we'd like to take a moment to recognize the rampant alcoholism in the restaurant industry. Too many talented and beautiful lives in the front of house and back of house are lost to alcoholism. We in no way support abusing alcohol and encourage you to respect it and yourself throughout all your days. We raise the collective glass to all of you. To late nights and bright futures! Cheers.

CONVERSION CHARTS

BARTENDER MEASURES		
Bar Measurements	Standard	Metric
1 dash	0.03 ounce	0.9 milliliter
1 splash	0.25 ounce	7.5 milliliters
1 teaspoon	0.125 ounce	3.7 milliliters
1 tablespoon	0.375 ounce	11.1 milliliters
1 float	0.5 ounce	14.8 milliliters
1 pony	1 ounce	29.5 milliliters
1 jigger	1.5 ounces	44.5 milliliters
1 cup	8 ounces	237 milliliters
1 pint	16 ounces	472 milliliters
1 quart	32 ounces	946 milliliters
1 gallon	128 ounces	3.78 liters

▶

U.S. Volume Measure	Metric Equivalent
⅛ teaspoon	0.5 milliliter
¼ teaspoon	1 milliliter
½ teaspoon	2 milliliters
1 teaspoon	5 milliliters
½ tablespoon	7 milliliters
1 tablespoon (3 teaspoons)	15 milliliters
2 tablespoons (1 fluid ounce)	30 milliliters
¼ cup (4 tablespoons)	60 milliliters
⅓ cup	90 milliliters
½ cup (4 fluid ounces)	125 milliliters
⅔ cup	160 milliliters
¾ cup (6 fluid ounces)	180 milliliters
1 cup (16 tablespoons)	250 milliliters
1 pint (2 cups)	500 milliliters
1 quart (4 cups)	1 liter (about)
U.S. Weight Measure	**Metric Equivalent**
½ ounce	15 grams
1 ounce	30 grams
2 ounces	60 grams
3 ounces	85 grams
¼ pound (4 ounces)	115 grams
½ pound (8 ounces)	225 grams
¾ pound (12 ounces)	340 grams
1 pound (16 ounces)	454 grams